IMPRINT
OF THE RAJ

Chandak Sengoopta grew up in Calcutta, where he qualified in medicine and psychiatry. He then moved to the United States, obtaining his doctorate in the history of science from Johns Hopkins University. Formerly a research fellow at the Wellcome Institute for the History of Medicine in London and lecturer at the University of Manchester, he is now Senior Lecturer in the History of Medicine at Birkbeck College, University of London.

D1514004

KA 0421083 2

IMPRINT OF THE RAJ

How fingerprinting was born in colonial India

CHANDAK SENGOOPTA

PAN BOOKS

THE LIBRARY

UNIVERSITY OF
WINCHESTER

First published 2003 by Macmillan

This edition published 2004 by Pan Books
an imprint of Pan Macmillan Ltd
Pan Macmillan, 20 New Wharf Road, London N1 9RR
Basingstoke and Oxford
Associated companies throughout the world
www.panmacmillan.com

ISBN 0 330 49140 7

Copyright © Chandak Sengoopta 2003

The right of Chandak Sengoopta to be identified as the
author of this work has been asserted by him in accordance
with the Copyright, Designs and Patents Act 1988.

All rights reserved. No part of this publication may be
reproduced, stored in or introduced into a retrieval system, or
transmitted, in any form, or by any means (electronic, mechanical,
photocopying, recording or otherwise) without the prior written
permission of the publisher. Any person who does any unauthorized
act in relation to this publication may be liable to criminal
prosecution and civil claims for damages.

1 3 5 7 9 8 6 4 2

A CIP catalogue record for this book is available from
the British Library.

Typeset by SetSystems Ltd, Saffron Walden, Essex
Printed and bound in Great Britain by
Mackays of Chatham plc, Chatham, Kent

This book is sold subject to the condition that it shall not,
by way of trade or otherwise, be lent, re-sold, hired out,
or otherwise circulated without the publisher's prior consent
in any form of binding or cover other than that in which
it is published and without a similar condition including this
condition being imposed on the subsequent purchaser.

UNIVERSITY OF WINCHESTER
WITHDRAWN FROM
THE LIBRARY

363.2500

In memory of Satyajit Ray and Roy Porter

Srabone mor nabo nabo shuniyechhile je shur tabo
Bina thheke biday nilo, chitte amar baje

Contents

Contents

Acknowledgements

Ever since hearing of William James Herschel and the colonial past of fingerprinting in Satyajit Ray's marvellous film *The Golden Fortress*, I had wanted to do something with the theme. Other commitments, however, kept getting in the way until recent conversations with Karen Fang and Ian Burney finally impelled me to write this book. Roy Porter, characteristically, offered inspiring suggestions on how to approach the project and with Natsu Hattori ensured that the finished work would see the light of day. That neither he nor Satyajit Ray lived to see it in print are tragedies I shall never cease to mourn.

Dan Todes, as always, was incomparable as mentor and friend, encouraging me to explore an area that many others considered to be rather dangerously far from my usual scholarly interests; Jon Agar repeatedly alerted me to themes and sources that I did not know would be relevant to the story; and Simon Cole was always willing to share his exhaustive knowledge of the history of fingerprinting, whether during a memorable evening at a New York tapas bar or via e-mail. David Arnold, Roberta Bivins, Indira Chowdhury, Waltraud Ernst, David Glover, Sarah Hodges, Shruti Kapila, Roy MacLeod, Greg Neale, and Punam Zutshi provided much encouragement; and Maurice Garvie helped me make sense of Edward Henry. It has been a joy to work with David Miller and Georgina Morley, who welcomed me into the world of 'real' publishing with warmth and enthusiasm. Everybody at Macmillan (especially Stefanie Bierwerth, Josine Meijer and Nicholas Blake, my desk editor) helped sustain that joy, and Neil Lang came up with a dust jacket that was simply perfect. Although the Wellcome Trust did not fund this research, it would scarcely have been possible without the support it has provided to me over the years.

My debts to libraries and archives – many of them old and beloved haunts, others glorious new discoveries – are immense. The John Rylands University Library of Manchester (especially its Document Supply Department and the ever helpful Store Supervisor, Joanne Crane), the British Library's Newspaper Library and the Oriental and India Office Collections, the Manchester Central Reference Library, the Manuscripts and Rare Books Department of University College London Library Services (in particular, Susan Stead), the Bodleian Law Library (especially Elizabeth Martin) and the Radcliffe Science Library, the Wellcome Library for the History and Understanding of Medicine, the Public Record Office, and the Bancroft Library of the University of California at Berkeley (especially David Farrell, Susan Snyder and Marilyn Kwock) went far beyond the call of duty to help me obtain elusive material. A special word of thanks is due to the superb Web version of the National Register of Archives of the Historical Manuscripts Commission: for a scholar trained before the flowering of the Internet, its powers to reveal the whereabouts of obscure manuscripts are nothing short of magical; warm thanks are also due to Michele Minto of the Wellcome Trust Medical Photographic Library for her assistance in obtaining many of the illustrations.

My sister Anuradha continued to be the rock of strength and support she has always been, as did Bappaditya Deb, Aniruddha Deb, Kanika Mitra, Paritosh K. Mitra, Aindrilla Mitra and Dipankar Mukherjee. Jane Henderson kept up my morale at moments of gloom, shared my joy when I found a rare document, got me many herself, presented me with the title, produced the index and still somehow found the time and energy to envelop me with love and warmth, even when I seemed to be declining into irreversible monomania in pursuit of the Belper Report.

List of Illustrations

UNIVERSITY OF WINCHESTER
LIBRARY

Picture credits

Courtesy of the Bancroft Library, University of California, Berkeley – 7, 12, 15, 23, 24; The British Library Newspaper Library – 26; Corbis – 19, University College London Library Services, Galton Papers – 8, 17, 20, 21; Wellcome Library, London – 1, 2, 3, 4, 5, 6, 10, 11, 13, 14, 18, 27, 28, 29.

Reproduced from Francis Galton, *Finger Prints*, London 1892–9, 16.

Reproduced from E.R. Henry, *Classification and Uses of Finger Prints*, London, 1901–22, 25, 30.

INTRODUCTION

A South London Burglar Makes History

It was just another day at the Old Bailey on 13 September 1902, with yet another series of boring and sordid cases. The accused was a forty-two-year-old labourer named Harry Jackson, charged with burgling the residence of Charles Driscoll Trustin at 156 Denmark Hill and stealing billiard balls on the night of 26 June 1902, and stealing 'plate and other articles to the value of £120' four days later from another local resident.

Prosecuting Jackson was Richard Muir, an eminent Treasury counsel of the day, who would later gain great prominence as the prosecutor of Dr Crippen. Normally, of course, a man of that stature would not touch a case so utterly unimportant. But only the alleged crimes and their perpetrator were uninteresting: the evidence that was going to be placed before the jury was historic. It was, Muir declared, 'of a kind which, so far as he knew, had never yet been used before a jury in an English criminal court'. He was referring to fingerprints.

When the burglar broke into Mr Trustin's billiard room, the window frames had just been repainted. The police found the fresh paint smudged by what looked like finger impressions. Sergeant Charles Stockley Collins, an expert at the Fingerprint Bureau established barely a year before at New Scotland Yard, came down to examine the marks, which were indeed fingerprints. Hoping they were the burglar's, Collins photographed them and searched his files for a match. The collection of criminal fingerprints at the Yard was nowhere as large as it would become but luck was smiling on the Bureau. A set of prints was found in the records that matched the marks left on the window frame at Denmark Hill. The hunt for the burglar's identity was over – but the man still had to be caught.

The police continued to be lucky. The actual man was arrested eleven days later for an unrelated incident, his fingerprints told their tale and Harry Jackson was charged with the Denmark Hill burglary. This was the magic of fingerprints: prints enabled the police not simply to record identity but to trace the criminal career of convicts. Jackson's was the first case, however, in which this new technique would face an English court. Would a British judge and jury accept it as valid? The technique was novel in Britain, police experience with it was minimal, the public knew nothing of it, and even the average judge or counsel knew little more than the public. It was fingerprinting itself that was on trial at the Old Bailey that day, rather than a mere burglar. Securing the conviction of Harry Jackson would secure the status of the remarkable new procedure – but how to convince the jury that the procedure was indeed as reliable, as foolproof, as the police believed it was?

Edward Henry, the energetic Assistant Commissioner of the Metropolitan Police and the guiding spirit of the Fingerprint Bureau, went all out for victory. Persuading Muir to prosecute was a coup but even that eminent counsel knew little about the nature of fingerprint evidence or its technique and significance. Henry and Sergeant Collins did their very best to train him, spending many hours coaching him on the basics of fingerprinting. Whether by chance or by design, Jackson's trial was presided over by Frederick Albert Bosanquet, the Common Sergeant of London, who had recently served on a Home Office committee that had recommended the exclusive use of fingerprinting to identify criminals. The outcome remained uncertain, of course, but with Muir briefed in detail, with Collins as the expert witness and with Bosanquet as judge, the Yard was confident that its case – and, far more important, the reputation of its new technique – could not lie in better hands.

Collins and Muir excelled themselves in explaining to the court the fundamental principles of identification by fingerprints. The ridges and furrows everyone had on their fingers, the jury was told, formed patterns that were unique to each individual and persisted through life. The chances of one man having the same ridge pattern as another were simply negligible. It followed that a man's – or a woman's or for that matter, a child's – finger mark was the ultimate form of identification, a true, lasting and unchangeable signature that could be easily obtained and retained on a piece of paper. Fingerprints could be used to identify anybody but their greatest value was in identifying criminals. A criminal might change his name, residence or appearance but he could never change the pattern of his finger-prints. A stray thumb mark found at a scene of crime could be as good as – indeed, far better than – finding the criminal's home address scrawled next to the corpse. The jury was then shown enlarged photographs of the finger impressions found at the scene of crime, those on file at the Yard, and those obtained from Harry Jackson himself after his arrest. 'This matter of finger-prints', Muir declared, 'had been reduced to an exact science'.

The prisoner did not believe a word of it. Representing himself, he challenged Collins to fingerprint him in court, so that the jury could compare it with the specimens on view. Collins was only too willing but the Common Sergeant did not permit the procedure. 'I can conscientiously take my dying oath that I know nothing about the burglary at Denmark Hill, and, therefore, the finger-prints could not have been mine,' declared Jackson. Unmoved, the jury returned a guilty verdict, at which the prisoner suddenly changed his tune. 'Be merciful, your lordship,' he begged. 'Give me another chance. I mean to get an honest living in the future.' His Lordship was not in a forgiving mood. 'It is clear', he announced, 'that you are a professional burglar, and the sentence upon you is that you be kept in penal servitude for seven years.'

As Jackson vanished into jail, fingerprint identification marched into British life and law. Sergeant Collins sent Jackson's fingerprints to the eminent scientist (and, as we shall see, passionate advocate of fingerprinting) Francis Galton, who published them in *Nature*, then as now the leading British scientific journal, emphasizing the practical value of fingerprints and urging their routine use in police investigations and matters requiring firm identification.

By the end of 1902, the Fingerprint Bureau had determined the identities of 1,722 suspected criminals. Within a few years came the sensational, widely reported Deptford case, in which two brutal murderers were identified by a fingerprint found at the scene of crime. Finally, in 1909, the Criminal Appeal Court ruled that a court or a jury might accept 'the evidence of fingerprints though it be the sole ground of identification'. Less than a decade after the establishment of the Bureau, fingerprinting had become indispensable to police work in Britain. Behind that historic change, however, lay a tangled history of hunches, debates, dead ends, uncertainties and negotiations. Colourful, unpredictable and still insufficiently known, the story cries out to be told.

Perhaps the most striking point about fingerprinting is that all the preparatory work that led to its adoption by the British police was done not in Britain, nor anywhere in the West, but in Bengal, a province of India, whose main city, Calcutta, was the capital of British India until 1911. It is a common assumption that all innovations in the heyday of Empire originated in Britain itself, from where some of them were transferred to the colonies, usually in diluted or distorted forms. The colonies dangerous pollution of the water in the higher interests of the public health.

The work is a welcome addition to public health literature, and it is sure to meet with general appreciation. It should appeal to a wide circle of readers, for it is written in a manner which presents a most important subject in a clear and intelligible light to everyone.

Nature Study : Realistic Geography. Model based on the 6-inch Ordnance Survey. Designed by G. Herbert Morrell, M.A. (London : Edward Stanford.) Price 5s.

THIS is a model of the country round Streatley-on-Thames, constructed by cutting out pieces of cardboard according to the contour lines and placing them one above another in the positions shown by the map. Spare pieces of cardboard, on which the contour lines are printed, ready for cutting out to make a second model, are enclosed in a portfolio along with the first. The construction of models of this kind has been carried out for some years in a number of schools, both in this country and abroad, but the general experience seems to be that, like the trigonometrical survey of the school and playground, and other similar devices, the time necessary to carry them out is too much for the value of the results obtained. The use of Mr. Morrell's model undoubtedly saves some time, inasmuch as the contour lines are already traced, but we suspect that the tracing of the contour lines is really the most important part of the exercise. But anything which assists in familiarising British school children with the ideas of contour lines and surfaces is to be welcomed ; it is astonishing how many children who are familiarly acquainted with isobars, isothermals and "iso-" lines of all sorts have scarcely heard of contour lines, and it is not too much to state that the failure to present the conception of a contour or "iso-" line as the intersection of a surface with the surface of the earth is almost the fundamental defect in our teaching of advanced physical geography. Apart from its application to the purpose for which it is immediately intended, Mr. Morrell's model should be of value to teachers for demonstration.

A Junior Chemistry. By E. A. Tyler, B.A. Pp. viii + 228. (London : Methuen and Co., 1902.) Price 2s. 6d.

THE author's primary object seems to be to enable boys to present themselves successfully for the examinations in chemistry held in connection with the Oxford and Cambridge locals and similar examinations. He recognises the existence of a better way of teaching his subject than the one he adopts, and urges in extenuation of his procedure the inadequate provision made for practical science in most secondary schools and the small amount of time devoted to science in them. Mr. Tyler expresses the hope that the book he has written will enable boys in ordinary schools "to acquire, as far as possible, a scientific knowledge of chemistry," but he does not seem to understand that science is not properly included in the curriculum because of the information its study imparts, but rather as a means of developing a habit of mind. Unless chemistry is studied experimentally, and is made to train the pupil to observe and to reason from his observations, it has no right to a place on the school time-table. Before the pupil has been set to study the preparation and properties of a few simple substances, and from his own deductions taught to discover the laws of chemical combination, Mr. Tyler tries to explain to him the atomic theory, Avogadro's law, compound radicals, and other theoretical considerations. Though the author understands well enough all the chemistry a boy need learn at school, he does not quite appreciate why men of science desire such subjects as chemistry to be introduced into school work.

LETTERS TO THE EDITOR.

[*The Editor does not hold himself responsible for opinions expressed by his correspondents. Neither can he undertake to return, or to correspond with the writers of, rejected manuscripts intended for this or any other part of* NATURE. *No notice is taken of anonymous communications.*]

Finger Print Evidence.

BY the courtesy of authorities in Scotland Yard, I have just received duplicates of two enlarged photographs (on slightly different scales). These photographs were lately submitted in a court of law to prove the identity of *a*, the mark left on the window frame of a house after a burglary had been committed, with *b*, the impression of the left thumb of H. J., a criminal then released and at large, whose finger prints are preserved and classified in Scotland Yard. I wished to show the resemblance between *a* and *b* by the method described in my "Decipherment of Blurred Finger Prints," believing that to be the readiest way of explaining to a judge and jury the nature of the evidence about to be submitted to them. I send the results. The questions of the best mode of submitting evidence and of the amount of it that is reasonably required to carry conviction deserve early consideration, for we may have a great deal of it before long. It is as a contribution towards arriving at a conclusion that I send the enclosed. I should say that in the above-mentioned book, each pair of impressions was printed in triplicate and on a still larger scale than these. One of the three was untouched, the second had lines drawn like those in the figure, down the axes of the ridges, the third had the lines and numbers and nothing else, just as in the figure. The attention

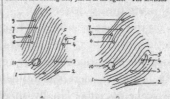

of the judge and jury could be easily directed by counsel to whatever pair of corresponding points he might desire, by reference to their common number on the chart. Without some such guidance it would be extremely difficult to do so, for persons unaccustomed to finger prints are bewildered by the maze of their lineations.

Certain more or less faint lines run across *a* that seem to have been made with the brush when painting the window frame. They seriously interfere with the lineations just above No. 5 and to the right of it. No. 5 is itself so far affected by them that I do not attach full weight to it as a point of reference. But accurate comparison is possible at nine other points, all of which are marked, and a close agreement will be found between every pair of them as well as in the number of intervening ridges. FRANCIS GALTON.

[The prints have been too much reduced from the tracings I sent, to be quite clear. Thus unless a lens be used, No. 2 in *b* will probably be misinterpreted.]

Remarkable Fossil Oysters from Syria.

IN examining a series of more than one hundred specimens of *Ostrea* (*Exogyra*) *flabellata*, Goldfuss, from the Middle Cretaceous of Lebanon, I was struck with the marked reproduction in the free upper valves of the figures of other shells to which the lower valves have been attached. These specimens were all collected in the same place, a hill near Bhamdūn, Mount Lebanon, Syria. They have been freed by weathering from a soft marly rock exceedingly rich in fossils. Specimens of Ostrea, Plicatula, Pecten and Anomia have the shell well preserved. Many others, including species of Cardium, Trigonia, Corbula, Isocardia, Cytherea, Leda, Nucula, Cerithium, Alaria, Melo, Pterocera, Turritella, Natica and others are preserved only as casts. Consequently the shell to

---

FIGURE 1

Francis Galton's letter to *Nature* on the fingerprint evidence in the Harry Jackson case.

provided many raw materials for British advances, to be sure, but little more. As the eminent French historian Elie Halévy put it in his magisterial *History of the English People in the Nineteenth Century*, Britain, by the end of the nineteenth century, had come to regard itself as the town 'with its offices, counting houses, and factories' and its far-flung colonies as the countryside producing the 'foodstuffs and raw materials needed by the mother country'. A closer look at imperial history shows how simplistic such stark distinctions are. The empire was, above all, a network of people, ideas and communication – and the traffic on that network could move in either direction. Every schoolchild knows that Britain gave its colonies the railway and the telegraph. It is recalled rather less often that it got curry, fingerprinting, and Worcestershire sauce in return, each of which has outlived the telegraph and, given the state of things in today's Britain, might even outlast the railway.

Not that the imperial innovations incorporated into British life were copied faithfully from indigenous ideas and practices. While indigenous inputs could certainly be crucial, a product of Empire was rarely completely British or indigenous. The nine-teenth-century curry powder, for instance, was indebted to spices used by Indians and could not conceivably have evolved in the British Isles. But it was not a replica of some indigenous Indian product – Indians brought up on recipes using variable amounts of freshly ground spices would consider such a fixed-proportion, ready-mixed combination to be an abomination. Developed in India but not indigenous, British but not evolved in Britain itself, the humble curry powder, created by imperial synthesis, incorporated into British tradition and then gradually re-transmitted to the world at large, blurs the simplistic distinctions we often make between home and Empire. So, perhaps surprisingly, does the history of fingerprinting.

Richard Muir was conscious of the importance of this imperial history and emphasized it proudly at the Old Bailey. The technique, he declared, was 'of the greatest importance in the admin-istration of the criminal law, and was now being introduced into this country on a very large scale for the purpose of identifying habitual criminals, as well as being applied to the detection of individual crimes. The system had had an extensive trial in our dependency in India'. Although not entirely forgotten, this imperial history of what became the fundamental proof of identity has never been delved into in sufficient depth. That is a pity. By exploring how fingerprinting originated, what purposes it served in the Empire and how it eventually came home to Britain, we can appreciate, I believe, not only the complexities of the history of this epochal technique of identification, but gain clearer, fuller, and richer insights into the ways in which Britain's imperial adventure transformed the lives not simply of the colonized but of the colonizers themselves.

ONE

The True Measure of the Criminal?
Identification before Fingerprints

Nineteenth-century Europe was a haven for criminals. Life was becoming steadily more urban, anonymous and mobile – in the large cities, one could simply disappear into a milling crowd of individuals and take on new identities that the surveillance and policing methods of the time could never hope to detect. As the historian Alain Corbin puts it, 'until about 1880 a clever person could change identities at will. He could obtain a new birth certificate simply by knowing the date and place of birth of the person whose identity he wished to usurp. Only an unlikely encounter with a witness who knew the person in question could thwart this subterfuge, and recognition based solely on visual memory could easily be contested'. Such a situation, it was widely believed at the time, could only lead to more crime, riots (perhaps even revolution) and, ultimately, total collapse of the moral and social order. The only effective way to control a mass of people was to control its individual members, but in order to do that one had to know *who* those individuals were.

Nobody, however, had yet evolved a foolproof method to establish a person's identity. The documents and procedures that existed were far from adequate and the police had no dependable way of verifying the identity of people they arrested. Was a man caught for purse-snatching a hardened old offender? In France, convicts had been branded until 1832, but after the end of that practice the police had no irrefutable identification.

An urban criminal's past was essentially inaccessible to the police unless the suspect was personally recognized by a policeman or a witness. There were no records that one could consult for a truly definitive answer. There were forms, to be sure – long, detailed, but of remarkably little use. French policemen were even trained to record a person's hair colour or any prominent identifying marks or disabilities but they were not trained to record them in clear, standardized ways, store them as easily searchable records, and retrieve them speedily when confronted with a person who might be pretending to be another. No experienced policeman relied on the forms, anyway: they were simply a tedious requirement. In the 1870s, photographs were added to the police records of a criminal but again, these were far from standardized in format – gentlemen, for instance, were photographed in hats – and were of little use for identifying a criminal who might have changed his appearance radically. Nor were these photographs indexed: they reposed in immense, unwieldy and practically unsearchable piles. Small wonder, then, that the police of the time did not have excessive faith in photographs: one well-known French method of identifying repeat offenders was, in fact, to assign an officer to greet prisoners on their arrival at the prison as old friends 'in the hope that this unexpected geniality might betray the prisoner into some admission that he had been in prison before'. Since officers were paid five francs to identify such recidivists, there was ample scope for corruption: bent officers often lured prisoners to admit to a previous conviction for a share of the reward.

The British police did not have a system of monetary rewards but the situation was not substantially better than in France, though concern with habitual criminals was no less intense. One journalist defined them as 'those who make crime a profession, the men who have proved their determination to fight against society, and who form a class which is responsible for by far the larger proportion of the law-breaking of the land'. In 1829, one writer proclaimed that thieves 'are born such, and it is their inheritance: they form a *caste* of themselves, having their peculiar slang, mode of thinking, habits and arts of living'. Such anxieties about a distinct class of hardened, incorrigible criminals became acute from the 1840s, when transportation of criminals to Australia ceased and the law-abiding British subject lost his earlier confidence that the worst criminals would be permanently removed. Around the same period, the growing threat of Chartism ensured that the concept of the dangerous class fused gradually with that of the rebellious poor. Intractable poverty and invincible criminality were supposed to characterize a self-contained and self-perpetuating dangerous class that was wholly separate from, although living within, the nation. In 1851, the Leeds reformer Thomas Plint claimed that over a third of all urban crimes were committed by this specific 'criminal class'. 'May it not be said of the class', he asked, 'that it is *in* the community, but neither *of* it, nor *from* it? Is it not the fact that a large majority of the class is so by descent, and stands as completely isolated from the other classes, in blood, in sympathies, in its domestic and social organization . . . as it is hostile to them in the whole *ways and means* of its temporal existence?' In his classic 1861 survey, *London Labour and the London Poor*, Henry Mayhew asserted that 'there is a large class . . . who belong to the criminal race, living in particular districts of society; the generations being born, and handed down from one age to another . . . until at last you have persons who have come into the world as criminals, and go out as criminals, and they know nothing else'. The cities of Britain, people increasingly felt, would soon be at the mercy of this ruthless enemy within.

Later in the century, with the police securely established and revolutionary threats having receded considerably, this hysterical attitude gave way to more focused fears. In his comprehensive study *Life and Labour of the People in London*, Charles Booth soothed Victorian nerves by declaiming that 'the hordes of barbarians of whom we have heard, who, issuing from their slums, will one day overwhelm modern civilization, do not exist. There are barbarians, but they are a handful, a small and decreasing percentage: a disgrace but not a danger'. Increasingly, it was one particular kind of malcontent that preoccupied the police: the habitual criminal or the recidivist, the criminal who was persistent, incorrigible, and unstoppable and for whom life imprisonment was the only appropriate punishment. Many theories of the hereditary nature of recidivism circulated at the time in England, including some that were reminiscent of or directly derived from theories of the Italian criminologist Cesare Lombroso, who taught that the 'born criminal' was a reversion to the earlier stages of evolution and could be identified by such distinct physical characteristics as a massive jaw or a misshapen skull. The police might believe in Lombroso's bizarre theories but they were of little use in catching *individual* habitual offenders.

What was needed was a foolproof system whereby a specific prisoner could be identified as having committed other crimes – the shape of his jaw might indicate that he was a 'born criminal' but that was not enough. Moreover, although misidentifications of innocent people as old lags were actually quite rare, there was still much concern about the occasional incident of an innocent person being labelled a recidivist. A Home Office committee argued in 1894 that the introduction of an improved system of identification would not only identify real recidivists accurately but also prevent misidentification of innocent people or first-time offenders as habitual criminals. To decide definitively whether an offender was a *repeat* offender, a recidivist, it was essential to have precise records of identification, which would reveal that an individual under custody had previously passed through police hands.

Even if one ignored crime and criminals altogether, the importance of identification was demonstrated by the sensational 1871 case of the Tichborne Claimant. Was Arthur Orton indeed Roger, the son of Lady Tichborne, and the heir to the Tichborne estate? Lady Tichborne was convinced that the claimant's ears 'looked like his uncle's' and over eighty witnesses agreed with her. But after a six-month trial, the claim was dismissed and Orton jailed. Photographs and portraits of Roger Tichborne had figured at the trial but failed to shake the faith of those who believed in Orton's claim. An even more dramatic illustration of the need for a dependable system of identification was the notorious Adolf Beck case, a classic of mistaken identity in British jurisprudence. In 1877, a man known as John Smith was convicted at the Old Bailey for introducing himself to successive women 'of loose character' as a nobleman (Lord Willoughby was one of his favourite monikers), inviting them to become his mistress, installing them in a house in St John's Wood and then absconding after having pilfered their money or jewellery. Smith was sentenced to five years' imprisonment and released in 1891. In December 1895, a similarly defrauded woman encountered Adolf Beck on the street and denounced him to the police as the man who had robbed her. Beck refused all knowledge but was identified as Smith not only by several other defrauded women but also by the police constable who had originally arrested Smith in 1877.

Sentenced to seven years in jail, Beck was treated as a repeat offender. He petitioned the Home Office several times but only in 1896 did the mandarins take the trouble to examine John Smith's records. They found to their consternation that the prison doctor had reported in 1879 that Smith was circumcised, which Beck, on examination, was found not to be. So Beck's 'previous conviction' was struck out but his current conviction was left untouched. He was released in 1901, but was arrested again on similar charges in April 1904 and re-convicted. The judge, however, postponed sentence, and in July that year Smith was arrested for acts that were shown to be committed whilst Beck was still in prison. This led to Beck's release and pardon for both his convictions with an award of £5,000 as compensation for the miscarriage of justice. A committee of enquiry, headed by the Master of the Rolls, investigated the whole saga, concluding that evidence of identity based solely on personal recognition was unreliable.

By the time the committee investigated the Beck case it was 1904, and as it noted approvingly, a reliable system of identification was then in use which might well prevent the repetition of such a calamity. But in the 1870s, when the Tichborne case was fought, or even in the 1890s, when John Smith was released from prison, there was no way of identifying individuals except through personal recognition by others. There was no system based on precise data that could pronounce incontrovertibly on a person's identity, regardless of who he claimed he was and who other people considered him to be. All Britain had in 1871 was the Alphabetical Register of Habitual Criminals, which was published annually and had been founded only in 1869. At first, it included every person convicted of felonies and certain kinds of misdemeanour – this, predictably, proved to be too large an undertaking and most of the 35,000 people added to the register every year could not be defined as habitual criminals. From 1879, the Register listed the names (arranged alphabetically), personal descriptions, distinctive bodily marks, photographs, details of previous conviction and destination on discharge of only those criminals with previous convictions and of every convict released from penal servitude. This was supplemented by the Register of Distinctive Marks, which classified the identifying marks on bodies of criminals. There were nine main groups – head and face, throat and neck, chest, belly and groin, back and loins, arms, hands and fingers, thighs and legs, feet and ankles – which were subdivided into categories such as, for the arms, 'loss of arms', 'tattoo marks', 'distortion from fracture or dislocation' and so forth. Theoretically, then, if a policeman suspected that an unknown man with a tattoo mark on his left arm might be a recidivist, he might verify his hunch by looking under 'arm, left' and then under 'tattoo marks' in the Register of Distinctive Marks, where he would find a list of all prisoners released that year with such marks and detailed descriptions of those marks. With a successful hit, the policeman could then proceed to the Alphabetical Register of Habitual Criminals and find further information about his suspect.

These registers should have worked well in theory but proved seriously wanting in practice. Even those policemen who consulted them frequently admitted that the information in the registers led to relatively few successful identifications. Some important police forces – such as the Metropolitan Police – tended to ignore the registers altogether but they had cumbersome registers of their own. Scotland Yard's Convict Supervision Office maintained various records, including an index of each prisoner's modus operandi and an unwieldy album of photographs (containing nearly 100,000 portraits in the early 1890s, which, on average, required about eight hours for each successful identification) of all convicts arranged according to age and stature of the individuals and the type of crime committed. Many county and borough forces had their own specialized registers.

This was an inefficient and often nightmarish system. First of all, the way the registers listed the distinctive marks was not detailed enough and the format did not permit the descriptions to be more exhaustive. Since the registers were not cumulative, each volume contained information pertaining only to those convicted during the year. To make matters worse, the annual registers were always published late – so the police often did not have any data on a habitual criminal for months after his release from prison, the very time when, according to authorities, he was liable to reoffend. Searching the registers could take hours, especially because they were not indexed precisely enough.

Consequently, many policemen still preferred to rely on identification by personal recognition. Convicts released on licence had to report to the police every month and through this, as well as through experience, policemen acquired some skill in facial recognition. As long as a habitual criminal indulged his habit within one particular district, the local police had little difficulty in identifying him, except in the most populous areas – most notably London, the anonymity and wealth of which made it attractive to a vast number of criminals, 'where an offender might be arrested in a dozen police divisions and convicted in a dozen different courts, without being seen twice by the same officer'. It was, therefore, the practice to house all prisoners remanded in London in one prison – Holloway – where they were inspected three times a week by thirty police officers and warders from all divisions of the Metropolitan Police and the City of London Police. The idea behind this was that an unconvicted prisoner, who was unknown to the officer arresting him, might turn out to be a familiar figure to one of the visiting team – perhaps an officer who had arrested him for a previous offence. It was considered a very effective method of identifying recidivists by the police: in 1883, for instance, 1,826 repeat offenders were identified by this exercise, 1,711 in 1888 and 1,949 in 1893. There was, however, a price: each successful identification by this method cost a total of ninety hours of detectives' time.

This system, in any case, was in use only within London. The county and borough forces used the 'route form' instead. Considered effective by their users, the route forms carried photographs and descriptions of prisoners whose past convictions the police wished to discover. Five or six police authorities which might have encountered the prisoner before were listed on the form and they constituted the 'route' travelled by the form. (In some cases, route forms might be sent to every police force in the country.) One after another would receive the form, and at each stop the prisoner's description would be scrutinized by as many members of that force as possible, and then the form would be forwarded to its next recipient with notes on previous convictions or the stark 'not known'. The last police force on the 'route' returned the form to the originating force, the whole process taking usually a week, which was the usual time for a remand. Although the police had faith in route forms, administrators worried about the total amount of time spent on studying the forms and were prepared to welcome a dependable substitute that consumed less official time.

In British courts, the proof of identification was 'always dependent on personal recognition by police or prison officers', observed a committee appointed by the Home Secretary in 1893 and chaired by the civil servant Charles Edward Troup (later Sir Charles Troup, Permanent Under-Secretary of the Home Office from 1908 to 1922). Although mistaken identifications were rare, a large number of recidivists were thought to slip through the system, especially in London. Sir Robert Anderson, the head of the Criminal Investigation Department, had admitted in 1891 that the legislation for habitual criminals was 'almost a dead letter'. In 1893, only fifty-five recidivists had been taken to court. 'Even with more photographs and more exact descriptions', Charles Troup's committee declared a year later, 'we are agreed that the present system will leave much to be desired. What is wanted is a means of classifying the records of habitual criminals, such as that, as soon as the particulars of the personality of any prisoner (whether description, measurements, marks, or photographs) are received, it may be possible to ascertain readily, and with certainty, whether his case is already in the register, and if so, who he is. Such a system is not, we believe, attainable merely as a development of the existing English methods'.

An effective identification system depended not simply on precision, but also on ease of retrieval. The best identification system in the world would be useless for police purposes were it not easily searchable. Since concern with recidivism was extraordinarily high in France, it is no surprise that the first really dependable method of criminal identification was developed in bustling Third Republic Paris, supposedly the mecca of every kind of malcontent – from burglars to anarchists, from rioters to sneak-thieves, from assassins to saboteurs. The new system was the brainchild of a police clerk named Alphonse Bertillon (1853–1914) and it spread rapidly to other nations, including Britain and its Empire. Before the advent of fingerprinting, it was the policeman's best friend and society's greatest guarantee against that worst group of offenders who went on a lifelong spree of crime safe in the realization that their careers could never be meticulously tracked by existing police methods.

Born to an eminent father (who was a doctor, a pioneer demographer and an anthropologist), Alphonse Bertillon seemed in his youth to be destined if not for a life of crime, then at least for one of utter futility. Uneducable, uncontrollable and frequently unbearable, he was the despair of his teachers and nicknamed the Barbarian. Although keen on collecting and arranging botanical and natural-historical specimens, he seemed to possess no other talent. After being expelled from several schools (including one dedicated to the education of difficult children), he finally displayed some thirst for knowledge when, bored to tears by compulsory military service, he enrolled on an elementary medical course. Fascinated by the human skeleton and its dimensions, Bertillon subsequently developed a keen interest in his father's profession of anthropology and, through his influence, was soon appointed as a clerk in the *premier bureau* of the Prefecture of Police in 1879. Predictably enough, he hated the job. Unpredictably, though, he stuck it out – and, as it happened, eventually attained an international renown that would be envied by no less a celebrity than Sherlock Holmes himself. In *The Hound of the Baskervilles*, when referred to as the 'second highest expert in Europe', Holmes asks frostily who might be the highest. The answer: 'To the man of precisely scientific mind the work of Monsieur Bertillon must always appeal strongly'. (In reality, it was Bertillon, as his biographers report, who admired the 'analytical genius' of Sherlock Holmes. And Holmes, in spite of professional rivalry, had great respect for Bertillon, once lecturing Watson at length on Bertillon's system during a train journey and expressing 'his enthusiastic admiration of the French savant'.) How and why had the apparently undistinguished Bertillon achieved such fame?

When he started working as a police clerk, some seven or eight thousand francs were being paid every year, Bertillon later recalled, to policemen as reward for recognizing criminals. Although this system managed to identify some fifteen hundred criminals, 'the magistrates and prison directors admitted that more than half of the habitual criminals arrested escaped recognition'. Now, although he was far from well educated in the conventional sense, Bertillon was an anthropologist's son. Nineteenth-century anthropology was preoccupied with physical measurements – it measured bodies with an obsessive thoroughness. The bodies of different races, of course, but also those of people within the same society who were suspected of being of a different kind, of being outside the norm represented by the white, middle-class, male scientist. Bertillon's father and his associates in the Society of Anthropology could not live without their measuring calipers and the child Alphonse, indeed, had spent many a happy hour playing with such instruments.

As he filled in form after routine, useless form at his desk, Bertillon dreamt of producing a system of measurement that would differentiate every human being from another. The surly clerk astounded his colleagues by developing a strange habit of cutting out specific features from photographs and then mounting pieces from different individuals 'side by side on pieces of cardboard'. The other clerks thought his mind was going, and when they learnt that he was assembling material for a report to the Prefect, they felt their diagnosis had been confirmed. But the report did go in – it was October 1879 and Bertillon had been in the job for a mere eight months.

The body of each individual, Bertillon had realized, was unique in its shape and size. The key to reliable identification of individuals lay in measuring bodies and tabulating those measurements systematically, not in gazing upon people's features and trying to memorize them. All the cutting and pasting of photographs had led to the evolution of a system that, he claimed, could produce a record that was 'the essential portrait of the person described and none other'. In order to determine the identity of an individual, one required eleven precise measurements of bony parts of the body. These measurements were the height of the individual, the length and breadth of his head, span of his arms, height whilst sitting, the width of the cheek and the lengths of the left middle finger, the little finger, the foot, forearm and the right ear. These had to be determined systematically with accurate calipers and rulers and recorded on a standardized card. The point was to measure those parts which were primarily bony and whose dimensions did not greatly change in adult life.

Even this set of eleven measurements, however, was not sufficient for identification. As Bertillon realized, measurements could never *prove* that somebody was the individual described on the card. A perfect match in measurements made identity strongly likely but it did not demonstrate it beyond all conceivable doubt. (It has been suggested that Bertillon was sceptical about the conclusiveness of measurements because he never fully grasped the mathematics of probability. If only he had increased the number of measurements to, say, fourteen, the chances against making a mistake in identity would then have

RELEVÉ

DU

SIGNALEMENT ANTHROPOMÉTRIQUE

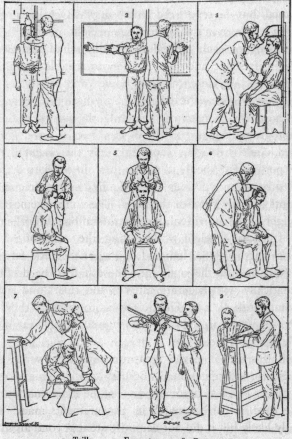

1. Taille. — 2. Envergure. — 3. Buste. —
4. Longueur de la tête. — 5. Largeur de la tête. — 6. Oreille droite. —
7. Pied gauche. — 8. Médius gauche. — 9. Coudée gauche.

FIGURE 2

Measuring the criminal by the Bertillon method.

risen to 268,435,456 to 1, odds that would have made identity practically irrefutable.) Whether due to ignorance of probability or the disinclination to increase the number of measurements, Bertillon added to the measurements what an admirer described as 'the deadly second barrel of his system'. Each measurement card would also have a physical description in standardized terminology and a list of specific identifying marks such as warts or scars.

Using such marks was nothing new, of course – but what was unprecedented was the language of those descriptions and sheer obsessive precision of the terminology used to describe the location and character of physical peculiarities. Bertillon worked hard to develop a precise, universal vocabulary for every feature of the body, from hair colour to facial wrinkles, from the beard to the voice, from the lips to the inclination of the shoulders, from the shape of the nose to the dimensions of warts and above all, the ear, which a historian has felicitously called 'the jewel of Bertillon's morphological vocabulary'. Each ear had to be described minutely on the Bertillon cards under four heads – border, lobe, antitragus and folds – each of which could be of several precisely named varieties.

Scars and marks had their own formulae: the description *Sc ov of 2.2/1.3 sl x at 6 bl elb bk fa*, for instance, signified an oval scar, 2.2 centimetres in length and 1.3 centimetres in breadth slanting externally at 6 centimetres below the elbow joint on the back of the forearm. Finally, all of this information could be abbreviated in accordance with a standardized scheme evolved by the originator – and transmitted, if need be, by telegraph. Together, these standardized records of an individual's physical appearance, characteristics and peculiarities constituted what Bertillon called a *portrait parlé*: a speaking portrait that described a person to the last detail and in terms that were precise, standardized, amenable to being learnt by heart, and of being transmitted purely in words.

Figure 3

A Bertillon anthropometric fiche with mugshot and measurements.

Planche 33.

Tableau synoptique des formes de nez.

1. — Nez à profil cave - relevé.

4. — Nez à profil rectiligne - relevé.

7. — Nez à profil convexe - relevé.

2. — Nez à profil cave - horizontal.

5. — Nez à profil rectiligne - horizontal.

8. — Nez à profil convexe - horizontal.

3. — Nez à profil cave - abaissé.

6. — Nez à profil rectiligne - abaissé.

9. — Nez à profil convexe - abaissé.

FIGURE 4

The different forms of nose described in Bertillon's
standard terminology for identification.

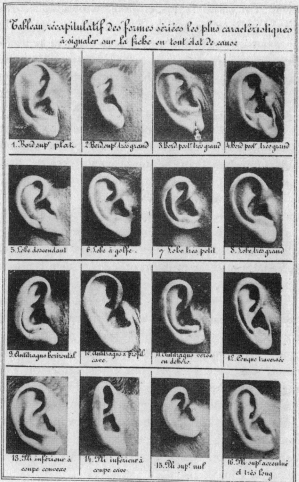

FIGURE 5
'The jewel of Bertillon's morphological system':
the different forms of ears.

To make his system completely watertight, he added a third component: the photograph. Bertillon's photograph, however, was not the police photograph of yore. An accomplished photographer himself, he appreciated that in order to be useful for identification, photographs had to be taken in well-conceived, standardized ways that would highlight all the facial features crucial for identification *in the same way* in *every portrait* of *every individual*. Every anthropometric card was to have a full-face and a right-profile photograph of the subject: it was Bertillon who introduced the classic mugshot. The profile photograph was more important than the full-face shot because, Bertillon explained, 'the silhouette of the forehead, the nose, and, above all, the ear, give an unalterable form'.

So far, so good – but the collection of information was only half the job. The challenge was to file all this data in an easily accessible – and compact – form. Bertillon himself declared that 'the solution to the problem of judicial identification consists less in the search for new characteristic elements of individuality than in the discovery of a method of classification'. His system of anthropometric measurements was a brilliant technical achievement but his filing system was truly a work of genius. The simplest but perhaps the most revolutionary innovation was the use of separate cards, rather than bound volumes as was the case with the British habitual criminal registers, thus permitting any amount of ordering, subordering, reordering and quick flipping through. But what was the best arrangement, one that would be most conveniently and rapidly searchable? Bertillon began by separating the cards of males from those of females. Then, for each sex, he made the deceptively simple assumption that all bodies and all bodily parts could be classified as large, medium, or small. Assuming that he was classifying a total of 90,000 cards, he began by taking the head as the primary part, dividing *all* the cards into three groups (of roughly 30,000 cards each) according to the length of the head – large-headed (i.e. long-headed), medium-headed and small-headed. Each of these was subdivided into three groups of roughly 10,000 each – once again, large, medium and small – by the *width* of the head. There were now nine groups, each containing about 10,000 cards. These nine groups were subdivided into three groups each, according to the length of the left middle finger, giving a total of twenty-seven groups of about 3,300 cards each. Each of the twenty-seven groups was further divided into three groups according to the length of the left foot, giving eighty-one groups, each containing 1,100 cards – each of these was divided into three categories according to the length of the forearm. There were now 243 groups, each with 300–400 cards. This completed the primary classification. Bertillon's card cabinet had twenty-seven sections, each divided into three shelves, and each shelf containing three drawers (243 drawers in all), holding about 400 cards each.

Even 400, however, was not a small enough number for quick searching and easy retrieval. So, each of the 243 groups was divided into three further groups (of about 140 cards each) according to the height of the individual and the latter subdivided into three somewhat unequal groups according to the length of the little finger. Each of these groups was finally ordered by the colour of the eye (of which Bertillon recognized seven for classificatory purposes) into groups of about seven cards each, although, by now, the numbers were no longer equal and these last subdivisions might contain anywhere between three and twenty cards.

The classification was now complete but in order to 'eliminate even the remotest chance of error', Bertillon also recorded the length and width of the right ear, the height when sitting, and the span of the outstretched arms. These measurements appeared on the card but were not used to classify them.

Bertillon is often mistakenly supposed to have discovered the identifying value of fingerprints. He was actually fairly sceptical

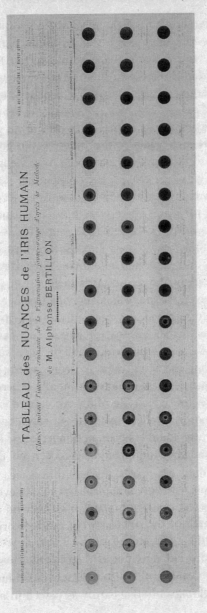

FIGURE 6
The eyes of Alphonse Bertillon.

28

about their importance, although, from the 1890s, prints of four fingers of the left hand were included on his cards, at the urging of the eminent scientist Francis Galton. But Bertillon's cards were always classified according to measurements – the fingerprints were there only to establish identity – except for juvenile offenders (whose bony parts were still developing and therefore unsuitable for measuring for identification purposes) and for women (whose measurements were considered to be uncertain, because of different hairstyles and 'recurring pathological disturbances'), where he used fingerprints as the sole basis of classification and developed his own system of classification for them. He was particularly interested in studying the special characteristics of the prints of people doing particular kinds of jobs: 'Seamstresses showed punctured prints on the left hand if they were right-handed, and vice versa. Florists had punctures upon all the fingers ... Continued contact with alkaline water wore down the ridge-marking on the fingers of laundresses ...' In 1902, he even identified a murderer from fingerprints left at the scene of crime, the earliest conviction for homicide in Europe on fingerprint evidence.

What Bertillon denied, however, was that fingerprints were so distinctly variable that they could be used as the *sole* basis for the identification and classification of 'several hundred thousand cases'. He argued that when matching prints, the identity of prints could be misleading – which he illustrated with some explicitly 'tweaked' prints. The only truly irrefutable evidence prints could offer was that of difference. In other words, dissimilar prints from the same digits could never belong to the same person, but the assumption of identity on discovering a number of similarities between an incomplete print and a complete one could be misleading.

Bertillon, therefore, preferred to rely on his own system and it certainly was a comprehensive one. Each individual's data were recorded in duplicate – one card was placed in an alphabetical register according to name and the other in the cabinet ordered by measurements. All the prisoners arrested in Paris were brought to Bertillon's department every morning and if they gave a name and admitted to having been measured previously, their card was found in the alphabetical register. If the prisoner denied having been measured, then his eleven measurements were taken immediately (and other identification marks recorded) and the anthropometric register searched for another card with identical measurements and identifying marks. If one was found, then a recidivist had been caught – and this happened with great regularity. The old French practice of rewarding a police officer identifying a recidivist continued, but now an officer recognizing a criminal who had not been spotted by the new system was given double the amount, the entire sum being deducted from the salaries of the anthropometric operators. This fine, said Bertillon, ensured that his operators were 'pecuniarily interested in the good application of the system'. Whether because of the reward/fine scheme or not, the system did seem to work. By the early 1890s, it had identified hundreds of recidivists and anti-recidivist laws had been passed in France in full confidence that they could be enforced.

Each year, Bertillon's office received and classified about 15,000 measurements from Paris and about 70,000 from elsewhere in France. Out of 30,000 people measured in 1889, there were only four misidentifications of recidivists. 'The probability of being recognized at once by being "bertilloné" is thus', its creator boasted, 'equivalent to certainty, as far as it is possible for anything human to approach this ideal'. Such was the reputation of anthropometry amongst crooks that Paris, previously a haven for international pickpockets, was now – supposedly – free of them. 'They prefer now to remain of their own accord', reported Bertillon, 'in foreign capitals'. But, he added, anthropometry was spreading to foreign nations and 'our poor international thieves are seeing all European countries successively closed to them'.

The fame of the Bertillon system reached Britain late in the 1880s, initially through the efforts of Edmund Spearman, a retired civil servant who tried ineffectually to induce the Home Office to adopt the system. The government was soon to be hit with heavier ammunition. The Council of the British Association for the Advancement of Science resolved at its 1892 meeting in Edinburgh that

> considering the recognised need for a better system of identi-fication than is now in use in the United Kingdom and its Dependencies, whether for detecting deserters who apply for re-enlistment, or old offenders among those who are accused of crime, or for the prevention of personation, more especially among the illiterate ... the Anthropometric methods in use in France and elsewhere deserve serious inquiry as to their efficiency, the cost of their maintenance, their general utility, and the propriety of introducing them, or any modification of them, into the Criminal Department of the Home Office, into the Recruiting Departments of the Army and Navy, or into Indian and Colonial Administration.

Letters urging the adoption of anthropometry were sent to the Secretaries of State for the Home Department, Army, Navy, India and the Colonies. The War Office and the Admiralty declined to institute anthropometric identification, while the Secretary of State for India informed the Association that anthropometry was already being used in India on an experi-mental basis. (We shall explore this at some depth later because it was crucial to the emergence of fingerprinting as the system of criminal identification.)

No reply from the Home Office is on record but it was the Home Office that responded most constructively to the letter. In October 1893, the Secretary of State for the Home Department, Herbert Henry Asquith, appointed Charles Troup's committee to recommend the best system for apprehending habitual criminals. Members of the Committee (Troup, Major Arthur Griffiths, Inspector of Prisons, and Melville Macnaghten, Chief Constable of the Criminal Investigation Department of the Metropolitan Police) visited Bertillon's department in Paris and observed his work with great interest. What floored the Committee was Bertillon's classification. 'If', it reported, 'absolutely invariable and accurate measurements could be obtained, then from the measurements of any person the card giving his name and antecedents could be found in M. Bertillon's cabinet as certainly and almost as quickly as an accurately spelt word could be found in the dictionary . . . M. Bertillon has obtained a primary basis of classification as nearly perfect as possible'.

But essential as it was, a sophisticated and easily searchable system of classification was not sufficient in itself. Were the measurements used by Bertillon sufficiently precise and sufficiently distinctive so as to identify an individual beyond conceivable doubt? Surely there would be many individuals so close to the average measurements that their dimensions would be practically indistinguishable? 'Nature', Bertillon had proclaimed, 'never repeats herself. Choose any part of the human body, examine it, and compare it carefully with the same part of another person, and differences will appear, more or less numerous, as your examination has been more or less minute'. The Director of the Penitentiary Department of the French Interior Ministry agreed that Bertillon's system gave every human being 'an identity, a certain individuality, lasting, unchangeable, always recognisable, easily proved'. The British committee, however, would have none of it. The possibility of two individuals having identical measurements might be slim but could not be discounted.

There were, moreover, formidable legal problems in adopting the system in toto in Britain. 'In Paris every person arrested for any offence is at once subjected to the process of measurement and is sometimes photographed before being brought before any magistrate. It would not', the Troup Committee emphasized, 'be consistent with English ideas to entrust to the police an arbitrary power of measuring or photographing every person arrested without authority from a magistrate and without regard to the necessity for the purposes of justice of discovering his antecedents and character'. An anonymous reader of *The Times* later denounced the Committee's recommendation for limited introduction of the Bertillon system in Britain as 'opposed . . . to the sentiments and principles of Englishmen'. It may all 'answer very well', he explained, 'on the Continent where everyone submits patiently to the inevitable, but it would not do in England'. It seemed, too, that the system required far too many measurements and it was doubtful whether 'prison warders or police officers of ordinary intelligence' could measure people speedily and with the kind of accuracy demanded by Bertillon's system. Bertillon himself was emphatic that he had calculated the 'maximum of tolerable deviation' between different examinations of the same person: as long as the measurements did not exceed this deviation, they could be taken to identify the individual. This, however, was not enough to reassure the British Committee.

Still, Bertillon's classification scheme was so magnificent that the Committee did not want to do without it. Consequently, it recommended that only those measurements be taken that were least subject to error due to 'actual variations in the body and from want of skill in the operator': head length and width, length of left middle finger, length of left foot and length of left forearm. Bertillon's seven eye colours were rejected as too difficult to distinguish, the height because it could be 'altered by trickery', and the length of the little finger because its dimensions were closely correlated with the length of the middle finger and had little independent importance. The remaining three of Bertillon's measurements – the length and width of the ear, the sitting height, and the span of arms – were also quietly excluded but of course, even in Bertillon's own system, they were not used for classification. (Once put into practice, the British system reinstated the height and added a new measure: the width of the face between the highest points of the two cheekbones. Bertillon had never taken this measurement but later used it in his own system to replace the width of the ear.)

The measurements, in any case, would be used only to classify records. Positive identification of the individual would be based on fingerprint matching. The Troup Committee had spent much time investigating the use of fingerprints for identification, and Francis Galton, in his evidence and through his demonstrations of the technique, had persuaded the members that it was the easiest, most convincing and most reliable way of proving the identity of an individual. In its report, the Committee declared that it would have recommended fingerprinting as the sole system to identify recidivists but for one crucial problem. There seemed to be no way of classifying fingerprint patterns as precisely and reliably as one could classify Bertillon measurements. Galton demonstrated his own system of fingerprint classification but it was considered too complicated for use by non-scientists. Hence, the Committee recommended a quintessentially British compromise. The five anthropometric measurements would be supplemented by prints of all ten fingers and, as in Bertillon's own system, a precise record of the scars and other physical marks in standardized terminology, giving exact locations and measurements.

In liberal England, however, the measurement of every prisoner and suspect was inconceivable. Only those sentenced to imprisonment with at least one proven previous conviction were subjected to measurement, although the system was soon extended to all convicts sentenced to penal servitude or to imprisonment followed by police supervision. The measurements as well as prints would be taken in prison by warders and then classified and maintained in a central registry, which should be based in the Convict Supervision Office of Scotland Yard and have a scientific adviser to supervise the training of warders, deciding on the limits of 'small', 'medium' and 'large', and to provide instruction on the 'decipherment and classification of finger prints'. (Dr John G. Garson, former Vice-President of the Anthropological Institute and for many years an assistant in the Anthropological Department of the Museum of the Royal College of Surgeons, was appointed to this post at a salary of £600 per annum.) Photographs should be taken in all cases – with a clear profile shot showing 'the forms of the ear and the nose' – and filed with the measurements and prints. The measurements would make the records easy to search, the photographs would supply some evidence of identity, and finally, fingerprints would 'afford in most cases the scientific proof of identity, and, wherever the system is applied, will render a wrong identification practically impossible'. (Women were included, but in the case of juvenile offenders, to whom the Bertillon system was inapplicable, only the finger impressions were recorded and arranged according to Galton's classificatory scheme (pp. 205–12), which would have been too complicated to use in a larger collection.)

The new identification regime was designed to supplement the older methods for several years rather than replace them immediately. The Metropolitan Police were not exempted from regular visits to Holloway Prison and the Committee recommended that the various registers and route forms should be continued 'until gradually and naturally superseded by the new system'. There was, however, no supersession and the modified Bertillon system did not have much impact in Britain. Although 822 applications were made for a search of the Register in 1900, and 293 former convicts were thus identified, the police continued to rely greatly on the older methods of personal recognition, whether route forms or the weekly visits to Holloway.

UNIVERSITY OF WINCHESTER
LIBRARY

Many of the country's police forces did not use anthropometry at all and even the Metropolitan Police used it only 'when all other methods have been tried in vain'.

The British may have been right to be cautious. The principles of Bertillonage were fine, but in practice the system was subject to individual error and omission. And to the deficiencies of instruments: the slightest defect in a caliper could lead to an error greater than the tiny permissible margin and thus make the measurement useless for establishing identity. Leaving aside doubts about the capabilities of prison warders, there were also fundamental problems in adopting the anthropometric data on which Bertillon divided his cards into large, medium and small. What was small in Paris was not necessarily small elsewhere. Even in a (then) homogeneously white nation like England, the system had to be recalibrated at the time of its introduction in 1894: the British authorities believed that what Bertillon had defined as a 'small' head, for instance, was small only when compared to other French heads and the police used Francis Galton's data to adapt Bertillonage to Britain. And in India, where Bertillonage had been introduced as early as 1892, the Parisian system came up against the obstacle of race. Although the Indian police, as we shall see in a later chapter, introduced an anthropometric system of criminal identification before Britain did, some of Bertillon's fine classificatory distinctions (such as his seven eye colours) or some of the points used in his precise personal descriptions (such as differences in skin pigmentation) simply did not occur in a dark-skinned population and had to be eliminated. Troup's committee had taken due notice of the Indian experience, observing that considerable readjustments were necessary before 'adapting Bertillonage to the requirements of another country'. Sooner than the Committee suspected, the colonial police would eliminate the need for Bertillonage altogether and transform identification practices in the mother country.

TWO

An Empire of Knowledge

It was, of course, fingerprinting that would vanquish Bertillonage and become the cornerstone of criminal identification. As we know, the fingerprint revolution began in India, but perhaps the most interesting fact about fingerprinting was that in its initial years it had absolutely no connection with the identification of criminals, habitual or otherwise. It began, instead, as a purely administrative tool – and only *one* of the administrative tools – that the British developed in order to govern their vast eastern possessions. In order to appreciate what fingerprinting was meant to do and why it evolved in the way it did, we need to step back from the narrower history of the technique itself and ponder the broader context of the Raj that brought it into being.

Today, bathed in the rosy hues of nostalgia, the average Briton regards the Raj as a wonderfully exotic adventure, spiced with curries and nautch-girls, and sustained by the unquestioned might of the greatest nation in the world. For the average nationalistically inclined Indian, the tale, instead, is one of reckless, unashamed and brutal exploitation of India and her people by perfidious Albion. Both versions have their grains of truth but neither has much to do with reality as perceived by the hundreds of British colonialists who passed through the subcontinent for a couple of centuries or, for that matter, by their countless Indian subjects. Putting aside our personal views on the legitimacy or illegitimacy of imperial rule, and looking at the early days of the British imperial experience as a simple phenomenon, what is striking is how unprepared the British were for their role and how utterly insecure their position. This insecurity was political, of course, but also one bred by their sheer lack of knowledge of the land, its people, their languages and their mores.

Imagine, if you can, an Englishman stepping into the damp swamps of eighteenth-century Bengal. This Englishman, let us not forget, was just an average trader, propelled by greed and doubtless a spirit of adventure but otherwise not exactly the 'lord of human kind' the Briton seemed to be a century later when the Raj was at its zenith. Everything in the country was utterly new and alien to him. He could not identify half the flora and fauna, did not have more than a smattering of the local lingo, was clueless about the local religion, laws and customs and, above all, did not consider the indigenous people to be even fully human. Communication with these strange dark-skinned beings was essential (not for edification but for business) but was it even feasible with such exiguous knowledge? 'No people', the historian Victor Kiernan wrote memorably, 'is easily understood, and India has always been a separate world, hard for any outsider, Eastern or Western, to penetrate. It was a freakish destiny that brought it and England together'. But brought together they had been – and British survival and British profit depended upon knowledge of this alien domain and its inhabitants.

The British quest for power and wealth, therefore, was always a pursuit also of knowledge. Not knowledge for the sake of knowledge alone – assuming such a disinterested pursuit is even possible – but knowledge as the basis of security, power and profit. The East India Company was not simply a trading corporation and a virtual government – it was also a full-fledged knowledge-gathering enterprise staffed by active, if variably talented, learners, explorers and investigators. The Company did not have a cadre of professional scientists on its staff: the gathering of knowledge, its codification and its exposition were the tasks of full-time administrators. Of course, even in Britain itself, science at the time remained an amateur, gentlemanly pursuit. In India, it was equally amateur an activity but far from a hobby. Under the blazing sun of the Orient, besieged by the unknown and attracted by profit, the East India Company's employees pursued knowledge less as gentlemen than as tradesmen yearning, even if not always consciously, to be rulers. There were, to be sure, exceptions. Many of these early imperialists, more than occasionally, sought knowledge at deeper and more extensive levels than dictated by imperial dreams. But such efforts had to be conducted subtly and carefully – as far as the East India Company's merchant directors were concerned, the only kind of knowledge-gathering they wished to sponsor was that related to their commercial and administrative activities.

The acquisition of new knowledge began, predictably enough, with languages. The Fort William College established in Calcutta in 1800 merely institutionalized the private tutoring that East India Company merchants had been seeking out for years. The College brought somewhat more of an academic air to what was almost exclusively a training for business but it never became an institution of higher learning in our sense. Much original scholarship evolved out of the tradition established at the College and a small but impressive body of scholarly men did emerge in Calcutta – symbolized by the formation of the Asiatic Society, dedicated to the study of Indian languages, religions, social customs and history. It is even possible to link these early British initiatives with the later flowering of a new kind of literary and cultural elite among Indians. All such outcomes, however, had nothing to do with the primary objectives of the College or the Company and were often achieved by Company employees working in their own time. This was not too common: the employees of the Company were recruited in their late teens and had not even been to university. Many undoubtedly learnt a lot of what their contemporaries would accept as science, but this was done on a purely personal basis. The Company, of course, did not regard the cultivation of science as part of its remit and never sought to recruit staff with prior scientific training (such as it was in the Britain of the late eighteenth and early nineteenth century). Nor was the Fort William College supposed to impart scientific training. The intended purpose of the College was to train administrators, whose main tasks would be to assess and collect revenue and, in later years, to govern. It was only because those tasks could not be acquitted satisfactorily without a knowledge of local languages and customs that the College had been founded.

At another level, the British needed to chart India as a physical entity. Even in Britain itself, cartography was a developing art, and in India maps were few and limited to very small regions. The country as a whole remained unmapped, the vast distances uncalculated, the mountains, valleys and plains uncharted. Here, too, the British acted for reasons that were neither purely scientific nor altruistic. The Empire was still being conquered and military expeditions into the heart of the country were only too frequent. An army needed maps. Surveys of the land were crucial for victory. Then, when the steam age dawned and coal became a valuable resource, surveys of the geological riches assumed importance. The study of Indian plants was crucial, not because so many were unknown and needed to be added to the annals of Western science, but because so many – such as indigo – were good for business and so many others could substitute for medicinal plants imported from Britain at great cost for the treatment of the Company's soldiers and employees suffering from the countless enigmatic but virulent diseases that India seemed to guard itself with. There were many outcomes from these efforts to explore the physical features of India, including the awe-inspiring Great Trigonometrical Survey of 1818, which charted and measured a larger chunk of the earth's surface than any other survey anywhere in the world – including the British Trigonometrical Survey established in 1764. Less obviously impressive to us today but of great significance then was the compilation of 'medical topographies' of various Indian regions. These recorded the details of climate, landscape, vegetation, geology, diet, diseases and local medical practices of a region in the hope of explaining the different forms taken by diseases in India from those in Britain. The cause of science was advanced faithfully by such projects but also the cause of Empire. To know the physical contours of a land and its plants was as important as possessing it militarily and politically and to know the ways in which it could endanger the foreigner's health was to take the first step toward physical invulnerability. As Company rule stabilized and the collection of revenue assumed more importance than military activities, mapping the land and ascertaining its ownership generated a new, sustained effort to know the country that was as notable in its time as the Great Trigonometrical Survey, even though posterity has been more awed by the latter.

The Company was, of course, wound up in 1858 after the disastrous Sepoy Mutiny (which politically correct historians now call the Great Rebellion), and the British Crown became the direct ruler of India. The ensuing period saw many changes as well as numerous continuities with the days of Company rule. The question of race now assumed far greater prominence than ever before. India and its people had never been considered equal to the British – even though admiration for ancient Indian civilization was tolerably common, Indians as they were evoked no compliments – but in the nineteenth century, it became a virtual obsession to delineate and identify the nature of the Indian's racial and ethnic difference. The interest in difference was not new: in the late eighteenth century, however, British savants had endeavoured to analyse that difference in the light of India's ancient history. The study of Sanskrit texts would explain why Indians were so very different from the British and how different groups of Indians were related to other Indians. As the nineteenth century wore on, British interest in the ancient roots of Indian culture waned, giving way to a new, anthropological interest in charting the physical and cultural characteristics – all of them lumped together as *racial* characteristics – of the population. This apparently more 'scientific' approach was stimulated less by the demands of science than by the 1857 Sepoy Mutiny. This revolt of indigenous soldiers began, it was universally believed, when Hindus as well as Muslims felt insulted on being asked to load a new kind of cartridge, greased with the fat of pigs and cows, in their rifles after biting off one end of it. The pig was considered unclean by both communities and the cow was sacred to the Hindus – if the British were not familiar with that basic a fact, then it was obvious that they needed to do much more to acquaint themselves with the characteristics and beliefs of their subjects. Simultaneously, the Mutiny deepened the British conviction of the utter racial foreignness of Indians. Consequently, the 'scientific' study of race came to assume an extraordinary political importance to the rulers of British India.

Race was the master concept of the era – whether in India or in Europe – and the study of racial characteristics, it was believed, would lead to a truthful view of the world. George Campbell, Lieutenant Governor of Bengal, remarked in 1866 that 'this country, in a far greater degree than any other in the world, offers an unlimited field for ethnological observation and enquiry, and presents an infinity of varieties of almost every one of the great divisions of the human race'. The ethnological questions the British wanted to answer related to the physical peculiarities of Indians but also to their cultural peculiarities.

Photography and anthropometric measurements were used as extensively as interviews. The nineteenth century was the age of a certain kind of science in the West – the keynote of that science was measurement. Measurements were the key to knowledge and India offered so many more enigmatic things and bodies to measure and count than did the West. A recent historian has rightly pointed out that the British in India 'undertook a massive intellectual campaign to transform a land of incomprehensible spectacle into an empire of knowledge'. Tabulate, measure, classify – those were the watchwords of that campaign. Or, as Edward Said has put it, 'divide, deploy, schematize, tabulate, index and record everything in sight (and out of sight) . . . make out of every observable detail a generalization and out of every generalization an immutable law . . .'

Humans were not exempt – physical anthropology was considered good science in the nineteenth century and all the more appropriate to investigations of an exotic and racially diverse population. The body and society would illuminate each other in concert, under the benevolent gaze of the ethnologist. The physical and the cultural merged strikingly in the study of caste, that supposedly quintessential characteristic of Hindu India. Since the caste system was supposed to date from time immemorial and because members of a caste never married outside it, the anthropologists of the Raj found it perfectly logical to determine the characteristics of caste from the characteristics of the body. Castes, indeed, were races, or as close to being races as made little difference. Herbert Risley's attempt to determine the social order of the castes from measurements of the nasal angle was only one expression of that conviction. The government of Bengal financed the publication of his magnum opus, the two-volume *Tribes and Castes of Bengal*, in 1891, which was crammed with anthropometric measurements. India, as the British then observed and historians now emphasize, was the great 'laboratory of mankind' and it was the anthropological explorer who was going to crack its most profound and redoubtable mysteries. But as Risley himself noted, 'such a survey will be a help to a good government . . . instead of being a mere scientific luxury, as it might be in Europe, it was almost an administrative necessity in a country like Bengal'. In 1882, the government of India had agreed in principle to conduct an ethnographic survey of the whole nation. In 1901, this finally got off the ground, comprising an ethnographic survey of 'the history, structure, traditions, religions, and social usages of the various races, tribes and castes in India', supplemented by a separate anthropometric survey to measure and tabulate the physical features of the population. This enormous project was conducted by numerous investigators under the overall charge of Risley himself. We might recall the Great Trigonometrical Survey with greater admiration today, but in their time, the great ethnographic surveys were probably considered to be of equally majestic stature.

Also in the late nineteenth century began the great project to enumerate the people of India and tabulate their social and religious particulars. The Census of India had its origins in the early efforts of the East India Company in the eighteenth century to compile detailed rent rolls for the districts from which it collected revenue. These were supposed to be accompanied by relevant information on the trades, crafts and agricultural activities of the region. This information was collected and assembled only very patchily, however, and unsatisfactorily supplemented, as the Company acquired more territory, by the attempts of some administrators to record whatever was known of the history, the leading families, caste groups and economic activities of the annexed land. From the early nineteenth century there were sporadic attempts to enumerate the population of a given area – the figures were always estimates and unfailingly controverted by critics – and to record their social and economic details. It was only in 1871 that a nationwide census was attempted and this, characteristically, put as much stress on collecting and analysing details of caste as on actually counting the population. Again, the census was regarded as a tool to enhance administrative control over the realm. Denzil Ibbetson, an eminent scholar-official who contributed extensively to the 1881 Census, remarked: 'Our ignorance of the customs and beliefs of the people among whom we dwell is surely in some respects a reproach to us, for not only does that ignorance deprive European science of material which it greatly needs, but it also involves a distinct loss of administrative power to ourselves'.

Related to the development of the Census was the development of gazetteers – reference tools containing information on the land and populace of every part of British India. In 1820, Walter Hamilton had produced his modest two-volume work, *A Geographical, Statistical and Historical Description of Hindustan and the Adjacent Countries*. Based on published material, the *Description* was neither encyclopaedic nor particularly reliable. In 1869, W. W. Hunter proposed to the government that a series of volumes be devoted to recording the geographical, human and social particulars of every province of British India. Hunter sought to aid the administrator in his daily work rather than to collect information in the spirit of pure science. Nothing, he warned, was 'more costly to a Government than ignorance'. His proposed volumes would not be addressed, he emphasized, to the 'scientific inquirer' but compile 'brief and careful sketches, such as might be useful to practical administrators' by giving them dependable information on the land and people under their charge. The government approved Hunter's proposal in 1871, the year of the first nationwide census, and nine volumes of *The Imperial Gazetteer of India* appeared in 1881. Soon expanded into fourteen volumes, it was revised again in 1907, leading to twenty-six stout volumes crammed with data on every part of the vast subcontinent. Even in the 1907 edition, the majority of essays were contributed by officers of the Indian Civil Service and the contents proceeded, historian David Arnold points out, 'from the physical foundations of India, represented by its geology, meteorology, botany and zoology, through a survey of its human inhabitants, similarly compartmentalised into ethnology, language and religion, to conclude, as if with the highest stage in this evolutionary saga, with the departments of colonial administration (public health and police)'. The vertiginous complexities of Britain's vast empire in the East had at last been codified, organized and tabulated. The exotic, endlessly alien realm had long been subjugated physically, but now, at long last, it had been mastered intellectually, socially, culturally and, notwithstanding Hunter's reluctance, scientifically. The empire of might was now also an empire of knowledge.

But how complete was this knowledge? The innumerable closely printed pages of the *Imperial Gazetteer* told the administrator all about the country, its provinces and their diverse geographical, climatic and geological features. It had much to say on the people, and especially on their castes, providing anthropometric information on their different physical traits. To the British administrative mind of the nineteenth and early twentieth centuries, all of this was valuable information and the *Gazetteer* was a cherished achievement. Nonetheless, there was one reality of an administrator's daily existence that it could not help him with. This was the identity of individuals. Even the most detailed knowledge of the physical and cultural characteristics of each caste could not help one decide whether an individual member of a caste was pretending to be another one. To know a person's caste might well be useful but even if the detailed anthropometric descriptions of caste churned out by ethnologists were accurate and dependable, what differentiated one man from another within his caste? This was anything but an academic question. In a population that was semiliterate at best, even signatures were unavailable. Was the illiterate peasant who signed a contract with his caste mark really the man he claimed to be? If a party to a contract later repudiated it as forged, how did one decide whether the disputing party had actually entered into the contract? What if a pension-holder died and his place was taken silently by another? Long before and long after the publication of the *Gazetteer* and the many other handbooks that complemented it, these questions vexed the administrator. Historians have written much about the imperial motivations of colonial science but sciences such as ethnology or geology facilitated control only in broad economic or socio-logical terms. These forms of knowledge failed to reach that level where the day-to-day business of the empire was conducted. There, one needed to know *individuals*. How, then, could one obtain a permanent, easily retrievable, and correct record of the identity of an individual? Obviously, the Bertillon approach to anthropometry could provide this knowledge but it had not been evolved until the 1880s. Was it, in any case, practicable to apply such a skilled technique to people at large? As far as the identity of the general run of individuals was concerned, Bertillonage was unlikely to be a realistic option.

Assigning names to individuals – that, says a recent historian, was central to the colonial drive for knowledge. The British were bewildered on noting 'how often the same things are called by different names, and different things by the same names'. It was imperative to move beyond this chaos of identi-ties into a clear, well-ordered world where individuals – whether plants, animals, vegetables or human beings – would have one irrefutable name, where identity would be stabilized and organized into a reliable and verifiable scheme. Establishing the identities of individual Indians, however, was important not only to avert conceptual chaos or to improve administrative efficiency in a largely illiterate environment – the prime motive was to counter what virtually every British official considered intrinsic to Indians: the propensity to lie, deceive, cheat and defraud. These traits were especially marked, if British colonial authorities were to be believed, in Bengalis, the inhabitants of the very region where the British Raj was at its mightiest. Thomas Babington Macaulay, once an influential figure in Calcutta, had devoted one of his trademark purple patches to this very theme. 'What horns are to the buffalo', he had declaimed, 'what the paw is to the tiger, what the sting is to the bee, what beauty, according to the old Greek song, is to woman, deceit is to the Bengalee. Large promises, smooth excuses, elaborate tissues of circumstantial falsehood, chicanery, perjury, forgery, are the weapons, offensive and defensive, of the people of the Lower Ganges'.

While few, if any, could match Macaulay's florid rhetoric, one only has to look at a few treatises on law, crime, or forensic medicine to be convinced that the Indian was assumed to be not only mendacious but incapable of differentiating between truth and fiction, at least in the court, where the dishonesty of the Indian and particularly the Bengali was thought to reach its apogee. In his pioneering 1870 treatise on forensic medicine in India, the medical jurist Norman Chevers pointed out that views such as Macaulay's were helpful but only in the legal arena. (Chevers was no simple-minded racist and added that a 'close observation of the "night-side" of London and a diligent study of the police reports and the Newgate Calendar would afford any quick-sighted foreigner an equally dark picture of the British character'.) While 'natives' in general might be as good or as bad as people anywhere, Chevers was strongly critical of their qualities as witnesses, endorsing the 1866 opinion of an Inspector-General of Police that in India, 'perjury is the rule and not the exception' and reminding his reader that even the august Privy Council had been moved to comment on 'the lamentable disregard of truth prevailing amongst the Natives of India'. Another authoritative textbook of forensic medicine for India lamented in 1914 the 'untrustworthiness of so much native evidence' and 'the wide prevalence of false swearing and fabricating false charges'. Virtually in every case involving natives, 'more or less false evidence is given, whether it be from fear, stupidity, apathy, malice or innate deceit' and that evidence was 'generally supported by marvellously minute direct and circumstantial details'.

In 1899, Sir Edwin Arnold, translator of the *Bhagvad Gita*, had warned that even judges could go 'unwittingly and unwillingly astray' in India, seduced by 'the atmosphere of lies which in India clings like an evil mist to both sides alike and renders facts undecipherable and theories perilous'. A medical jurist echoed this in his 1908 analysis that the duty of a judge in India was 'not so much to decide which story is the true one and which the false one, but to separate the falsehood and the truth on both sides, and having eliminated the former, to decide upon the case . . . In England, the discovery that some of the evidence for the prosecution had clearly been concocted, would probably be quite sufficient to ensure the release of the accused; but if such a rule were to be followed in this country, there would scarcely ever be a conviction'. Civil cases were especially rich in perjured evidence and forged documents, usually on both sides. Such embellishments of evidence, the author was anxious to emphasize, were not always intentional 'and only requires a little patience and good humour to find out what is true and what is false'. In orthodox legal opinion, circumstantial evidence was supposed to be the best kind of evidence but the author found it astonishing how often in India, 'circumstances are forged so as to fit in with one another'. Trying hard not to slip into a blanket condemnation of Indians, he proffered a quasi-psychological explanation. 'The idea of a witness of the uneducated class of inhabitants, seems to be that he must help the judge to convict or acquit the prisoner, as the case may be', he suggested. George Otto Trevelyan, no Indian-hater by the standards of the era, remarked repeatedly on the mendacity and duplicity innate to the character of the Indian, and these traits, he believed, were accentuated by the native's ingratiating nature. 'A Hindoo never sticks at a lie, but in the witness-box he surpasses himself', he observed. 'The testimony of a single one of our countrymen has more weight with the court than that of any number of Hindoos, a circumstance which puts a terrible instrument of power into the hands of an unscrupulous and grasping Englishman ... The Bengalee witness, who has no motive to lie, will distort the facts if he imagines that he can by so doing give one tittle of pleasure to the barrister who is examining him, or the judge who is taking notes of his evidence'.

Chevers had summed it all up neatly long ago: 'In England, it may be taken, as a general rule, that all information, contributed in aid of medico-legal enquiry, contains nothing that can be regarded as a wilful misrepresentation ... There, men all combine, with earnest purpose and sharpened faculties, to reveal the hidden guilt. In India, however, the deceit inherent in the character of the lower class of Natives, surrounds all judicial investigations with an atmosphere of obscurity'.

Such views did not disappear with the end of the nineteenth century. If anything, the tone sharpened further, perhaps under the impetus of the growing nationalist movement. Sir Cecil Walsh observed in his 1930 book *Crime in India* that even 'the simplest and most straightforward cases are constantly tainted with palpably untrue statements and inconsistencies', revealing 'the duplicity and cunning, the indifference to human life, the callous indulgence in false evidence and false charges and the lack of moral fibre which daily manifest themselves among the millions of cultivators'. Also in the 1930s, a British medical jurist proclaimed that 'from the point of view of law, if Indians are left alone, those will win an action at law who are able to give the biggest backsheesh; that is the prevailing thing among the natives ... From my experience of the East, when an Englishman arrives there he is on his mettle'.

Knowing the land and its people, then, was integral to ruling them – but in order to rule such a duplicitous people, knowledge of languages, customs and general racial types was not enough. The identity of each individual subject had to be fixed and authenticated so that they could not give false witness, repudiate contracts, forge documents. Smooth administration of the colony – and impartial, honest and efficient administration was supposed to be the greatest British contribution to Indian history – depended on precise and unambiguous identification of individuals. Signatures were not the solution in India, photography was hardly practicable with the current state of technology and the financial resources that would be required and, although one actually encounters it less frequently in colonial discussions of identification than one might expect, many British administrators in India undoubtedly found the facial features of coloured people virtually indistinguishable.

The problems faced by European police forces in identifying habitual criminals was not only a later phenomenon, but it paled beside the sheer magnitude of the colonial problem of identifying every individual who might buy a piece of land, draw a pension, or sign some kind of contract. All the *Gazetteers* the administrator-savants could compile could not resolve it, nor could the most meticulous charting of the physical characteristics of caste. This was why systematic identification by fingerprints evolved in colonial Bengal rather than at the heart of London or Paris. It was certainly not the case that Europeans had never noticed the distinctiveness of fingerprints. As long ago as in 1684, the English physician and pioneer botanist Nehemiah Grew (1641–1712) had pointed out in the pages of the *Philosophical Transactions of the Royal Society* that the fingertips were covered by 'innumerable little ridges, of equal bigness and distance, and everywhere running parallel with one another'. The British engraver Thomas Bewick had used his finger marks in 1804 and 1818 to 'sign' his books on birds. Bewick's engravings, however, were resurrected as fore-runners of fingerprinting only after fingerprint identification had become a household concept. At the time, they caused neither surprise nor emulation. In 1823, the Czech physician and physiologist Jan Evangelista Purkyne (1787–1869) even classified fingerprints into nine different types – this, again, went virtually unnoticed at the time but was celebrated as a harbinger when the fingerprinting system was almost fully developed.

To notice a curious fact, however, is not the same thing as evolving a use for it. If necessity is the mother of invention, then the necessity to invent a scheme to identify individuals by some simple, indisputable marker was unimaginably stronger in the colonies than in Europe. Europeans, of course, had their anxieties about habitual criminals and other marginal people but these were almost negligible in comparison to the problems of identity and identification confronting colonial administrators.

THREE

'A Signature of Exceeding Simplicity'

Finger marks have been used as signatures since antiquity, especially in India, Japan and China. This, however, was not founded in the belief that the ridge patterns on the fingertips, being unique to each individual and persisting unchanged through life, could be used to record and verify an individual's identity. Ancient finger-dabs, as far as we know, were no more than signatures or personal marks. The modern fingerprint, on the other hand, is not just a signature, but a signature that can be attributed definitely, demonstrably and irrefutably to one specific individual and nobody else. The use of a thumb mark to sign a document is, no doubt, ingenious, but the use of fingerprints to record the identity of a person in a form permitting, by comparing an individual's prints with the recorded print, the conclusion that the two were made – or could not possibly have been made – by the same person is a different kettle of fish altogether.

Even if we focus only on the modern concept of fingerprints, it is far from simple to pinpoint its discoverer. Was it, for instance, Thomas Taylor, a scientist at the United States Department of Agriculture, who suggested in an 1877 lecture that the ridges on the palms and fingertips could be used to identify criminals 'by comparing the marks of the hands left upon any object with impressions in wax taken from the hands of suspected persons'? Or was it discovered by several people at the height of American anxiety over what seemed to be an endless influx of Chinese immigrants into California in the 1880s? American lawmakers and enforcers had sought an easy way of identifying Chinese individuals, all of whom seemed to them to look the same. The Bertillon system, at that point, was new even in Paris and American officials were yet to hear of it. (It was only in 1896 that there was an American proposal to use Bertillon measurements – this, too, was to identify the Chinese.) But some, unaccountably, had heard of fingerprints – it is not known from where but it is not impossible that the information had come from Chinese sources. In 1883, a California detective, Harry Morse, had suggested that Chinese immigrants be identified by thumb marks. Officials had ignored his suggestion but the Superintendent of the San Francisco Mint, Franklin Lawton, who was independently interested in using fingerprints as identifying marks, had approached the well-known landscape photographer Isaiah W. Taber to photograph thumbs and establish their identifying attributes. Taber himself, however, wrote that he became aware of the individuality of fingerprints when he had 'accidentally inked' his thumb and was struck by the impression left on a blotting-pad. He began to experiment 'with a view to using such marks for identification', and although the experiments do not seem to have numbered more than forty (he took the prints of about twenty Chinese and twenty white people), he nevertheless came to the conclusion that thumb impressions were always distinct and that the ridge patterns were not transitory. He sent photographs of thumb marks to the government, who did not respond, and the problem was resolved in 1888 when Congress forbade the entry of all Chinese labourers. Taber – motto: 'We mirror Nature' – remained convinced, however, that thumb marks offered 'a more reliable means of identification than portraits'.

Interesting as these efforts were, they had been preceded by the emergence of fingerprinting as a *routine*, *official* process of identification in colonial India in the 1850s and 1860s. This system did not survive in its original form for very long and it certainly did not appreciate the full potential of fingerprints (for the detection of criminals, for instance), but it was definitely the earliest comprehensive effort to institute fingerprints as markers of identity in the modern sense. It is not at all unlikely that the British 'discovery' of the procedure was influenced by ancient oriental traditions of signing with a finger mark, which had never died out. 'Much, certainly, is to be said for the influence of Eastern ways and customs', observed the pioneering historian of fingerprinting, George Wilton, 'in directing their [Europeans'] attention independently to the marvellous nature of our finger-tips ... Consciously or not, they evolved out of their Eastern environment their respective ideas and conceptions and applied these to the institution of fingerprint criminal registers and to the tracing of criminals'. As those remarks imply, however, only the initial inspiration may have been indigenous: the Western interest in finger impressions led to the evolution of a technique radically different in form and purpose.

The story of fingerprinting in the British Empire begins with the colonial civil servant William James Herschel (1833–1917), the scion of a distinguished scientific family. His grandfather, Sir William Herschel (1738–1822), discovered the planet Uranus in 1781 and his father, Sir John Frederick William Herschel (1792–1871), was a well-known astronomer and mathematician. Herschel's father, who referred to him as 'my unruly boy Bill', had requested him not to adopt astronomy as a career and the young man had decided, therefore, to go east. After a stint at Haileybury, the training college of the East India Company, Herschel left for Bengal when he was just twenty. He was first posted as Assistant Collector and Magistrate at Maldah, where his job 'involved trekking from village to village, and camping each night, in order to collect revenue dues and hold Courts of Justice under the banyan tree'. Bengal was not the scene of the

FIGURE 7
Sir William James Herschel, Bart.

most fierce battles of the Sepoy Mutiny of 1857 and Herschel complained to his relatives that he was 'missing the excitement'. After the Mutiny was over, however, many deserting sepoys trickled into Bengal and Herschel experienced some late excitement: once, he came across a group of forty-eight armed deserters but succeeded in disarming them 'by showing himself unarmed and promising pardons if the Sepoys laid down their arms at his feet'. The Mutiny, of course, led to the end of Company rule in India and when the British Crown took over, Herschel remained, now a member of the Indian Civil Service. His first major posting was at Jangipur, an obscure village in Bengal.

In 1858, he entered into a contract for the supply of road-making material with a local businessman called Rajyadhar Konai. (Jangipur was wild country and it was one of Herschel's jobs to have roads cut through the forests.) 'He was about to sign it in the usual way, at the upper right-hand corner, when I stopped him in order to read it myself', Herschel recalled more than half a century later. He felt the need to 'frighten Konai out of all thought of repudiating his signature thereafter'. Why this fear? 'My executive and magisterial experience had ... forced on me that distrust of all evidence tendered in Court which did so much to cloud our faith in the people around us', Herschel explained. 'We cannot be too thankful that things have greatly improved in India in the last sixty years, but the time of which I am speaking was the very worst time of my life in this respect. I remember only too well writing in great despondency to one of the best and soberest-minded of my senior companions ... about my despair of any good coming from orders and decisions based on such slippery facts ...' It was in this suspicious and insecure spirit – which, of course, was a pretty mild version of the British colonial distrust of Indians that we encountered in the previous chapter – that, all of a sudden, he thought he would ask the Bengali contractor to stamp the contract with a print of his right hand:

He, of course, had never dreamt of such an attestation, but fell in readily enough. I dabbed his palm and fingers over with the home-made oil-ink used for my official seal, and pressed the whole hand on the back of the contract, and we studied it together, with a good deal of chaff about palmistry, comparing his palm to mine on another impression.

Many have wondered just why Herschel thought of this particular procedure. Herschel himself observed dismissively that there was nothing very original about his idea: instances had long been known of the hand, or the nail or even the teeth being used to 'certify a man's act, or a woman's'. As a boy, he recalled, he had loved Thomas Bewick's work on birds, although he claimed that by the time he asked Konai for his handprint on the contract, he had forgotten all about Bewick's habit of affixing his thumb mark to his books. He also acknowledged that illiterate Indians used finger-dabs as signatures (called *tip-soi* in Bengali, the local language) but since those dabs were mere smudges without any identifying attributes, they did not, he asserted, inspire him to study the individuality of fingerprints. But even if he was wrong about this and it *was* the supposedly unidentifiable *tip-soi* that had induced him to explore whether more carefully taken finger marks might serve to record a person's identity, the use of the entire palm was still quite unusual. Soon, he had to make a second contract with Konai and asked him for the same signature. This second contract he sent to Francis Galton many years later with the following note:

So difficult was it then 1858 [sic] to obtain credence to signatures that I bethought me of the signature of the hand itself. It was the first idea that occurred to me of the kind, and was only intended to frighten the man. It was not the custom of the country to sign so – But purdanishin women [women living in seclusion – in *purdah*], when signing a document sign by dipping the tip of the finger in common

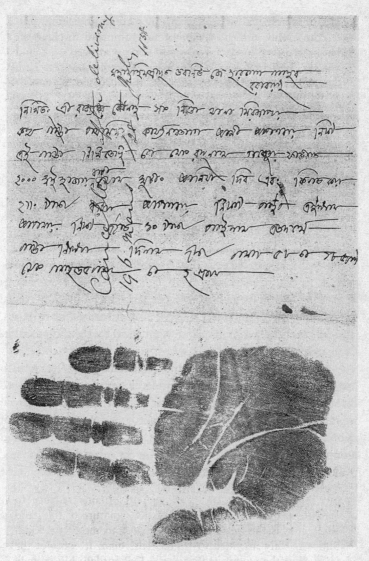

FIGURE 8
Herschel's original contract with Rajyadhar Konai.

ink and making a 'blot'. This is called teepsahi . . . and has no connection with the system of recognition by the lines of the skin.

The most exotic explanation for Herschel's brainwave has been offered by fingerprint expert and historian Gerald Lambourne. Herschel, he suggests, may have

> heard of, or witnessed, a Hindu suttee ceremony. Suttee was the ritual suicide of a widow on the burning funeral pyre of her dead husband. As she passed through the Suttee Gate on her way to her death the widow would dip her right hand in a red dye and place a print of the inside of it on the gate . . . Certainly the Konai handprint looks remarkably like a 'suttee' hand-print.

It is impossible to believe that Herschel would have forgotten such an exotic connection – there is no allusion to it anywhere in his many reminiscences of what exactly he did in 1858 – but the issue remains (and will probably always remain) so mysterious that even Lambourne's somewhat lurid speculation cannot be dismissed out of hand.

When Konai's handprint was published in 1916 in Herschel's historical pamphlet on fingerprinting, a battle was raging in Britain over who had first discovered the identifying characteristics of the ridge patterns on fingertips. The challenger to Herschel's claim, Dr Henry Faulds (of whom, more later), pointed out incredulously that all the finger-ends in Konai's print were mere dabs – the furrows were quite undiscernible. 'No identification could be effected on such a basis, and the system was therefore clearly *not* discovered in 1858 by the baronet', proclaimed Faulds. Herschel retorted that as he had recorded in the pamphlet, he had himself noticed this very fact in 1858 and proceeded to repeat the experiment with his own hand and fingers, soon deciding that, 'for securing a signature which the writer would obviously hesitate to disown', it would be more useful to use just the fingers. At this point, that was all he was interested in. He did not think of fingerprints as tools for *verifying* the identity of individuals and even in his thoughts on using the finger marks as signatures, he did not imagine that the ridge-patterns were so distinctive and so enduring that disowning them might lead to conviction for perjury. 'That was not settled', he observed with regard to the legal validity of identification by fingerprints, 'and could not have been settled, to the satisfaction of Courts of Justice, till, after many years, abundant agreement had been reached among ordinary people. The very possibility of such a "sanction" (to use a technical expression) to the use of a finger-print did not dawn upon me till after long experience, and even then it became no more than a personal conviction for many years more. The decisiveness of a finger-print is now one of the most powerful aids to Justice. Our possession of it derives from the impression of Konai's hand in 1858'.

Although Herschel may not have seen the future possibilities of fingerprint records immediately, he carried on doggedly collecting and studying their characteristics. He was indefatigable in collecting specimens from friends and colleagues and his 'fad' became well known wherever he was posted. Henry Cotton, who eventually became the Chief Secretary to the Government of Bengal and played an important role in introducing the official use of fingerprints in India, was first posted to the country as Herschel's assistant in 1867. He reminisced many years later that 'at this time, and for many years previously, Sir William Herschel was actively engaged in working up the system of identification by finger-prints. Acting on purely empirical lines, he lost no opportunity of experiment, and my own thumb impressions were taken by him often enough forty-three years ago'. Another civil servant colleague of Herschel's, John Beames, himself a highly accomplished linguist and no unimaginative civilian, did not go into detail but it is possible that he had Herschel's interest in fingerprints in mind when he recalled in his *Memoirs of a Bengal Civilian* that 'though a man of very eccentric habits [Herschel] was an extremely charming companion, full of reading of all kinds, a fascinating talker and a most enthusiastic worker'.

Although he never rose to the highest echelons of the British Indian bureaucracy, Herschel occupied a demanding post during a period of crisis. In 1860 – two years after his encounter with Konai – he was transferred to the district of Nadia in Bengal as a magistrate, a standard post in the Indian Civil Service, which was largely judicial and partly administrative. What were not so typical were the time and place of his posting. Nadia in 1860 was the nerve-centre of the so-called Indigo Rebellion, peasant revolts that were enormously important at the time and which, in Bengali tradition even today, dwarf the great Sepoy Mutiny of 1857 as an expression of popular discontent with colonial rule. That mythic stature is somewhat overblown but the history of these revolts is inseparable from the story of fingerprinting. Although the importance of this connection was acknowledged by Herschel himself and although it is mentioned in histories of the indigo disturbances in Bengal, it has never, to my knowledge, been noted, let alone seriously explored, by historians of fingerprinting. In order to explore the link, however, we need to know rather more about indigo cultivation in nineteenth-century Bengal than one might expect.

The indigo plant yields a blue dye that was in demand in Europe for, among other things, dyeing military uniforms until the introduction of aniline dyes in the early twentieth century. Indigo had been grown in India from antiquity (and even exported) and was one of the many exotic commodities that attracted the Portuguese, the Dutch and then the British to India. In the late eighteenth century, Joseph Banks, the President of the Royal Society and scientific adviser to the East India

Company, had urged its directors to turn India into a veritable plantation for the cultivation of sugar, cotton, coffee and indigo, all of which were profitable but none of which could be grown in Europe. So profitable was indigo that it brought the English East India Company four-hundredfold profits, and it was delighted to support its cultivation by providing advances to European planters. By the early nineteenth century, the indigo industry was flourishing in Bengal and the Company did not even need to pay advances to planters any more. The curious feature of indigo cultivation in Bengal was that although managed and marketed by European planters for their own profit, it was never cultivated in self-contained plantations. For many years, the Company did not permit planters to own any land for cultivation, partly because of fears that the planters (many hailing from the lower classes) would misbehave and antagonize the populace against British rule (which was yet to attain that illusion of permanence which it acquired by the end of the nineteenth century) and partly from anxieties that extensive landowning by individual Europeans might, in time, encourage them to attempt an American-style takeover of the Bengal government.

The prohibition on landowning by indigo planters was lifted later but indigo cultivation in Bengal never evolved a real system of plantations. Instead, the planters entered into contracts with peasants (called *ryots*), paying them advances to grow the plant on the land for which they had tenancy rights from local landholders (*zamindars*). The *ryot* did not earn much from growing indigo and frequently lost much – his economic survival was dependent on other crops that he sowed on his fields in addition to indigo – and as the nineteenth century wore on, the *ryots* grew progressively keener to abandon indigo and concentrate on more profitable crops such as rice. 'Virtually indigo and rice are in many places rival products, contending for land', acknowledged the government's own investigative commission into the Indigo revolts, 'and no doubt, at the present high prices for rice, and the late low rate paid for indigo plant, rice is more advantageous to the agriculturist'. It was not simply a question of profit either. The specific requirements of the indigo plant demanded accurate timing in sowing and reaping, immaculate weeding, and immediate transport to the factory for extraction of the dye after harvesting. The *ryot*'s job was an arduous one and ended only after he had delivered the harvested crop to the planter's factory, where other (usually Indian) staff processed it to obtain the dye. John Beames, who knew much about indigo cultivation from his experience in districts where it was grown, acknowledged in his autobiography that 'the work is hard and unceasing, as the pulp has all to be pressed before it gets dry. It is also much disliked on account of the loathsome smell of the wet indigo'. Building and running an indigo factory, however, were expensive propositions and planters, naturally, craved profits big enough to justify their investment. Their behaviour caused comment even amongst their own countrymen. As George Otto Trevelyan, who knew India well, would declare some years later, 'the ryots cultivated indigo under a system which, in the hands of shrewd and energetic European planters, had become an instrument of intolerable oppression'.

On the face of it, there was nothing inherently inequitable about the system of indigo cultivation. If anything, it looked enlightened for the time, in being based on contractual obligations, entered into by two independent parties of their own choice. In practice, however, indigo cultivation was one of the most disorganized, dishonest and oppressive activities of the British in Bengal – not only did it sour relations between the British and the Indians but it was one of the rare issues dividing the British themselves. In the annals of British India, the indigo disturbances followed the Sepoy Mutiny of 1857 but the battlelines were far more ambiguous in the former – so much so that on numerous occasions, it seemed as if the British Indian government was in battle with sections of British residents in India and that too, not for narrow political interests, but to protect the interests of Indian peasants. It is by no means a glorious episode of colonial history – there was too much collusion between planters and government officials in repressing the peasants – but nor can it be told purely as a nationalist tale, in which all the colonists were evil and unjust and all the indigenous actors sea-green incorruptibles. What, then, are the facts about the indigo disturbances and how exactly did they affect the history, of all things, of fingerprinting?

First of all, the *ryots* were not under the direct control of the planters and the two parties were always liable to disagree over predictable questions: Had sufficient indigo been produced and delivered to justify the advance paid by the planter? If not, was the advance going to be returned? How? Who, in short, would interpret the obligations of both sides and enforce the contracts? Also important was the position of the indigo planters: there were few Europeans in the interiors of the country, most being concentrated in Calcutta, the capital of British India. Apart from planters, the only Europeans in the backwoods were government officials and missionaries: the indigo planters often boasted that they had done more to permeate British influence into the interior of the country than the government had ever managed. In reality, however, their isolation generated a constant anxiety of being at the mercy of an indigenous peasantry and also encouraged a megalomaniacal disregard for the government's laws when such disregard was useful for business. The bullying of *ryots*, destruction of food crops and forcible sowing of indigo, countless acts of petty despotism and villainy – the kidnapping of refractory *ryots* and imprisoning them in factory godowns, for instance – were only too frequent. John Beames, one of the rare magistrates who stood up to planters, recounted this incident in his autobiography:

Now in the eyes of a . . . planter, a man who refused to grow indigo was a rebel, and a dangerous character and all measures were lawful against him. So Baldwin [a planter] sent men with ploughs, who ploughed up every inch of ground round the *ryot*'s cottage, sowed it with some coarse, cheap kind of pulse, put a fence of thorns round it, and so made the man and his family prisoners in their own house . . . The wretched man and his family trembled and endured for two days, but when their food supplies were exhausted and they could not go so far as their well to draw water for household purposes, despair gave them courage. Although there were men put to watch them, the *ryot* managed to slip out at night and hide till the morning when he came into my court and told his tale.

Beames summoned the planter to court and at this, the latter, 'who was as great a coward as he was a bully, got frightened and paid the man a large sum to compromise the case. He also removed the fence and ceased to molest the man'. The same planter later incurred Beames's wrath again for locking up three *ryots* for refusing to process indigo.

A broader problem involved the whole indigo trade. When European demand was high, as in the mid-1840s, the industry prospered, indigo contributing in some years almost half the value of goods exported to Europe from Bengal. When European demand fell, the indigo trade in Bengal suffered, often calamitously: in 1847, for example, there was a spectacular collapse, leading to the bankruptcy of many Calcutta business houses dealing in the dye. The indigo business, in short, was chronically unstable and unpredictable and the periods of prosperity, although dazzling, were always brief and never sustainable. The capricious weather of Bengal could reduce production even when European demand and prices were high. The *ryots* suffered if they could not produce enough indigo to repay the planter's advance and make a profit – if disturbances in weather, for instance, hampered production, then the peasant's investment in the crop could easily exceed the advance he had been paid by the planter. The planters' profits were harmed, too, but for a peasant living close to or below subsistence level, the fluctuations of the indigo trade could be cataclysmic.

The situation was worsened during the 1850s, when food grains from Bengal rose in demand, lowering the trading importance of indigo and the profitability of cultivating it. Peasants, understandably, wanted to get out of the indigo trade and grow grains instead: they were especially aggrieved because the best indigo was obtained from plants sown in April and harvested in the late summer, which was also the best time for rice cultivation. The government, too, was no longer keen on nurturing the indigo business, which it saw, not unjustifiably, as being less important than other crops as an article of international commerce. The interest of the planters, therefore, was threatened from two sides and it was this combination of peasant recalcitrance and the perceptible diminution in governmental interest that precipitated the indigo disturbances.

From the mid-1850s, petitions by disgruntled *ryots* against the planters were common in the indigo districts, and when, towards the end of the decade, Indian deputy magistrates supported the *ryots*, the planters saw red. An occasional British official also incurred the wrath of the planting lobby by upholding the *ryots*' complaints. The basic issue was one of the *ryots*' autonomy – if they did not wish to sow indigo, then could they be forced to do so? The rule of law in the countryside, of course, was represented by the British magistrates – who, no doubt, felt equally isolated in the countryside and were usually open to being courted by the planters (usually their only European neighbours), leading frequently to collusion with them in legal disputes with the *ryots*. Beames was an exception, but even he recalled that after the episodes recounted above, the planters of his district 'took to flattering and courting me, inviting me to their factories and showing me and my wife many civilities'. His predecessor in the post, however, had been, in Beames's doubtless diplomatic words, 'a good-tempered, easy-going fellow, extremely popular with the planters and, I have no doubt did his duty according to his lights. That was no affair of mine; I had to do my duty according to my lights'.

By the end of the 1850s, exceptional magistrates such as Beames had a champion at the highest level of the Bengal government. John Peter Grant, appointed Lieutenant Governor of Bengal (the head of the Bengal government) in 1859, was a true nineteenth-century liberal free-trader. Grant upheld the rights of the individual peasant and opposed the indigo planters because (and only insofar as) they interfered with the right of the *ryot* to cultivate what he wished to cultivate. The *ryots*, he asserted, were not 'Carolina slaves but the free yeomanry of this country and the virtual owners of the greater part of the land'. If the planter could not afford to pay the price of their labours, then it was the planter who would have to give way. Emboldened by this new attitude of the government, peasants in village after village began to rebel against the planters and refused to accept advances for growing indigo. The planters often sent in armed staff to force the *ryots* to do their will, and such forays often ended in pitched battles between the peasants and the armed enforcers. Allegations of forged contracts, abductions and forced sowing of indigo were rife, ably circulated by the Bengali press in Calcutta and energetically, often scurrilously rebutted by sections of the British press. The *ryots* received the support of some of the big landholders (the *zamindars*) and, more importantly, of the indigenous mass media of Calcutta, where a new liberal intellectual tradition merging Eastern and Western values was developing rapidly. These urban intellectuals were neither particularly close to the peasant population nor opponents of British rule. Most knew little of the countryside and virtually all of them accepted the Raj as the best available option. They did, however, consider it their right as well as their duty to criticize and oppose practices that they found abhorrent. The indigo system was one such.

The Lieutenant Governor did not entirely disagree with them. He ordered magistrates to remain neutral and enforce the law fairly – for which he was vilified by the planters and their supporters – and when that proved insufficient, promised to appoint a commission of inquiry into the indigo trade. It was only then that the disturbances began to subside. The Commission sat in Calcutta in May 1860; in July, it travelled out to Herschel's Nadia ('the district, where the dislike to sow had been most openly manifested') for additional hearings. In all, fifteen government officials, twenty-one planters, eight missionaries, thirteen *zamindars* and seventy-seven *ryots* were interviewed. The number of peasants who travelled down to Calcutta, eager to give evidence, astonished the Commissioners: 'They came, literally, in scores and hundreds from the districts . . . and, as it would have been impossible to take the depositions of even one-half of the number, a selection was made by ourselves, with due regard to variety of caste, and residence in particular factories or concerns; that is to say, Hindoos and Mohammedans, and even Christian *ryots* were examined'.

Investigating the indigo trade and its consequences from a broad range of perspectives, the Commission produced a 762-page report that was submitted to the Government of Bengal as well as to the British Parliament. Although the report did not discount the possibility that peaceful indigo cultivation might bring prosperity to the countryside, the nature of the existing system caused the Commission much disquiet. Its report declared many of the *ryots*' allegations of oppression to be well founded and rejected the planters' allegation that officials had unfairly sided with the *ryots*. The Lieutenant Governor considered the numerous instances of coercion and oppression revealed in the report to be 'a disgrace to the Administration'. Grant was not against indigo cultivation per se but simply in favour of free trade: any practice which infringed the seller's right to determine the price of his products was anathema to him. His understanding of justice, moreover, would not let him ignore the legitimate complaints of people simply because they were impoverished and supposedly belonged to an inferior, conquered race.

These principles were shared only very variably by the civil servants responsible for enforcing the law. One who did, as we have seen, was John Beames, then magistrate at Champaran. The planters suspected Beames of inciting the *ryots* but Beames calmly recorded in his *Memoirs* that 'I had not stirred up the *ryots* in any way, but they had long been dissatisfied, and finding they had at last a Magistrate who would do justice impartially between them and the planters, they judged the time opportune for rising and resisting their oppressors'. Another such honourable magistrate, and one whose efficiency and integrity were lauded by Indians of the time as well as by recent historians of the indigo disturbances, was none other than William James Herschel.

Transferred to Nadia as magistrate at the height of the disturbances, Herschel was in charge of investigating and deciding on the innumerable complaints of coercion, the vast majority of which turned on questions of identity. As he recalled in 1916,

The Indigo disturbances in the district had given rise to a great deal of violence, litigation, and fraud; forgery and perjury were rampant. The rent-rolls of the *ryots* put into Court by the *Zemindars*; the *pottahs* (agreements for rent) purporting to be issued by them to each *ryot*, put in by the latter; the *kabooliyats* (acceptances) purporting to be signed by the *ryot*, and tendered in evidence against him; all these documents were frequently worth no more than the paper on which they were written ... Things were so bad in this and other ways that the administration of Civil Justice had unusual difficulty in preserving its dignity.

The planters regarded Herschel as being excessively sympathetic towards the *ryots* but a more objective glance at his actions shows that he was simply against dishonesty on either side. As magistrate, he favoured summary punishment for anybody infringing a contract and never hesitated to rule against *ryots* when he considered them to be in breach of contract. He repeatedly warned the peasants that he would enforce contracts impartially and if necessary would call in the military police to aid him. The notion of the contract, of course, was sacred to Victorian law and Herschel was hardly unusual in his conviction of its sanctity. Where he stood out was not in his beliefs but in his practice. Whilst the average British magistrate in Bengal would doubtless have shared conventional ideas on the importance of contracts, he would also be only too happy to wink at contract manipulations, forgery, or infringement, when committed by a European planter. Herschel and Beames, however, were as implacable with Europeans as with Indian peasants. And that did not please the planters. As George Trevelyan noted, 'the theory that the native is his equal in the eyes of the law is of itself sufficiently aggravating to the European settler; but, when the occasion comes for that theory to be put in practice, when justice demands that one of our countrymen should be brought to account for outrage or oppression, then class hatred breaks forth into a paroxysm of illogical fury'.

Just as planters often forged contracts, Herschel clarified in his testimony before the Indigo Commission, many *ryots* repudiated genuine contracts and there was no simple way of ascertaining the validity of the pieces of paper submitted as evidence. When asked by the Commission whether he supported the idea of the registration of all contracts, Herschel assented, emphasizing, however, that where one of the parties was illiterate or semiliterate, registration alone could never be enough:

The only objection to registration is, that it does not secure absolute proof of the identity of the person charged with breach of contract, with the person who signed the document. If personification at the time of signature, or false pleas of personification afterwards, were rendered impossible by any peculiar mode of signature, nine-tenths of the difficulty of forming a decision would disappear, and with it nine-tenths of the process necessary to bring the trial to an issue. I can suggest a signature of exceeding simplicity, which it is all but impossible to deny or to forge. The impression of a man's finger on paper cannot be denied by him afterwards.

The Commissioners ignored his suggestion completely and even at the peak of his dispute with Henry Faulds over who was the first to appreciate the value of fingerprints in identification, Herschel never alluded to this brief but clear announcement of the unique attributes of finger marks, which had been made under oath, published in a document submitted to Parliament, and available, in theory at least, to all and sundry.

The exact reason why Herschel asked Rajyadhar Konai to sign his contract with the whole palm will remain mysterious for all time. What is clear is that his convictions on the value of fingerprints in identification were formed and reinforced by his experiences during the turbulent years of the indigo disturbances. 'I was driven to take up finger-prints now with a definite object before me', he would write in old age, 'and for three years continued taking a very large number from all sorts and conditions of men'. Before he left Nadia, the disturbances had subsided but the Courts were still 'choked' (as he put it) with lawsuits turning on the genuineness of contracts. 'I took courage from despair', he recalled, 'and in my judicial capacity (if I remember right) addressed an official letter to the Government of Bengal, definitely advocating administrative action to enforce the use of "finger-prints" by both parties as necessary to the validity of these documents'. The government remained silent.

Many years later, however, Herschel heard from a senior civil servant that the inaction had been motivated by the fear that the introduction of fingerprinting might well trigger a new controversy just when the indigo situation was improving. 'He added that it was a matter of regret now, that no action whatever had been taken, but he pointed out that legislation would have been necessary to make the new marks admissible in evidence, and to get such a law on the spur of the moment would have been hopeless. That difficulty had certainly never occurred to me when I made the suggestion . . . At the time I wrote it is quite certain that no Court in India, no pleader, no solicitor had ever recognized such signatures as these'.

Herschel's interest in fingerprinting and his determination to use it for administrative purposes did not, however, dissipate because of governmental inaction. He continued to collect prints and even worried whether they could be forged: he asked some of the best artists in Calcutta to imitate some specimen prints. The results were good but not identical and he felt confident now that their use for identification was eminently practicable. His 'hobby' became known even back home, where he indulged in it during his furloughs. And it was the support of his family, especially his sister, which impelled him to 'give the thing an open official trial on my own responsibility'. In 1877, Herschel – who had succeeded to the baronetcy in 1871 – was appointed the Magistrate and Collector of the Hooghly District, a stone's throw from Calcutta. Here, he had control over the criminal courts, the jail, and the Department for Registration of Deeds and was in charge of the payment of government pensions.

He began with the pensioners, many of whom, he suspected, had long ago died and been replaced by impersonators. As he put it delicately, the 'vitality' of pensioners had been 'a distracting problem to Government in all countries'. If impersonation was indeed common amongst the pensioners, then it is strange that he encountered no objections at all from them to the new technique. On the contrary, he reported that they gave him their 'glad approval' and he was especially anxious not to offend their religious sensibilities. 'The memory of the greased cartridges of the Mutiny ... was indelible ... I was careful, therefore, from the first ostentatiously to employ Hindus to take the impressions wanted; using, as a matter of course, the pad and the ink made by one of themselves from the very seed-oil and lamp-black which were in constant use for the office seals in the various departments'.

The next target was the Registration Department. Recent legal changes had mandated that signatures on deeds ('whether in full or by caste mark, or by cross, or in the case of women mostly, by touching the paper with the tip of the finger wetted with ink from the clerk's pen') had to be made in the presence of the Registrar, who was responsible for preventing imposture and relied on the 'sworn evidence of witnesses attesting their personal knowledge of the executant'. In spite of the new measures, however, impersonation still occurred and Herschel introduced fingerprinting into the registration process to prevent such attempts. 'After the legal formalities of registration had been observed, the Registrar made the person print his two fingers on the deed, and again in a diary book which was kept by him in the office, for my own inspection rather than as evidence'. Although the attempt succeeded brilliantly, he later heard of an interesting case of repudiation of a fingerprint in a neighbouring district, where a man had 'cut off the joints of his fingers, hoping to defeat justice by corrupting the witnesses so as to prove that he was *not* the man they had recognized before the Registrar'. The attempt was unsuccessful and he never heard of any other repudiations of a fingerprint that had been 'pressed to this bitter end in India or elsewhere'. The use of fingerprinting in registration of deeds was welcomed, he later reported, by 'every official and legal agent connected with these offices'. The new device 'lifted off the ugly cloud of suspiciousness which always hangs over such offices in India. It put a summary and absolute stop to the very idea of either personation or repudiation from the moment half a dozen men had made their marks and compared them together'. In a letter to his wife Emma, the devout Herschel exclaimed that fingerprinting was 'a miracle, a miracle from on High'!

He now turned to the jail, where, as he put it again with delicacy, unambiguous evidence of identity was 'not un-needed'. According to him, it was common practice in India for convicts to get others to serve out their sentences 'for a consideration'. An even safer but far more expensive stratagem was 'sham death and a purchased corpse, affording comparative safety after escape'. The use of fingerprinting in prisons, he believed, would enable random checks on prisoners' identities, making such substitutions impossible. Crime itself was not his major concern but the prevention of impersonation. So, he ordered that the fingerprints be taken of each offender at the time of sentencing on the 'records of the Court and also on the warrant to the jailer'. By this time, his health had broken down and he had decided to leave India for good. Nevertheless, he tried for one last time to induce the government to adopt fingerprinting.

He wrote long letters to the Inspector of Jails and to the Registrar-General describing his 'method of identification of persons, which, with ordinary care in execution, and with judicial care in the scrutiny, is . . . for all practical purposes far more infallible than photography'. He had gathered enough evidence over the years to assert unequivocally that the patterns of a fingerprint 'do not (bar accidents) change in the course of ten or fifteen years'.

His introduction of it in daily administrative work at Hooghly, he observed, had demonstrated the simplicity and practicability of the operation. 'The cogency of the evidence', moreover, was 'admitted by every one who takes the trouble to compare a few signatures together . . . I have taken thousands

RIGHT FOREFINGER OF SIR W. J. H. in 1860 and in 1888.

in 1860   in 1888

DISTRIBUTION of the PERIODS of LIFE, to which the evidence of persistency refers.

Persons.	Age at first print.	Interval in years.	Age at second print.	Ages, 0—80 years.						
				10	20	30	40	50	60	70
H. H—l	2	13	15							
A. H—l	4	12	16							
J. H—l	8	13	21							
E. H—l	10	12	22							
W. J. H—l	28	30	56							
R. F. H—n	26	21	47							
N. H. T—n	27	28	55							
F. H. H—t	27	26	53							
W. G—	62	17	79							

FIGURE 9

The unchallengeable evidence of persistence of fingerprint patterns: Sir
William James Herschel's impressions, taken twenty-eight years apart.

now in the course of the last twenty years, and ... I am prepared to answer for the identity of every person whose "sign-manual" I can now produce if I am confronted with him'. Emphasizing the larger value of the method, he added the common allusion to the Tichborne Claimant, which Faulds, too, would highlight: if, wrote Herschel, there had been a fingerprint of Roger Tichborne in existence, then 'the whole Orton imposture would have been exposed to the full satisfaction of the jury in a single sitting by requiring Orton to make his own mark for comparison'.

He urged the Inspector of Jails to use fingerprinting to verify the identity of prisoners. 'Call the number up and make him sign. If it is he, it is he; if not, he is exposed on the spot. Is No. 1302 really dead, and is that his corpse or a sham one? The corpse has two fingers that will answer the question at once'. Nor, he pointed out for the benefit of the Registrar-General, was the utility of the method confined to jails alone: it was such a simple and valuable technique that it could be used in a multitude of administrative contexts, especially amongst illiterate people, making 'a substantial contribution towards public morality'. Its use in Hooghly had succeeded so phenomenally that Herschel did not believe that 'the man lives who would dare to attempt personation before the Registrar here'.

The government, yet again, failed to show much enthusiasm for Herschel's technique. In a private letter to Francis Galton, he recalled that the Inspector of Jails had 'said he did not see what I wanted him to do'. Many years later in England, he met Sir James Bourdillon, who had been the Registrar-General at the time. Bourdillon remembered the letter clearly and declared that he had asked around for more information on Herschel's work but had then 'lost sight of the matter'. He had, however, always wanted to meet Herschel 'to express his constant regret at having let my suggestion slip through his hands'. The Inspector of Jails of the time, too, later confided to Herschel that he had no recollection of replying discouragingly to Herschel's letter and, in fact, had taken 'great interest in the Finger-print system of identification, of which I always regarded you as the Apostle in India'.

When Herschel left India, his work on fingerprinting was known only very superficially; even some of his greatest admirers did not necessarily know of it. On the eve of his departure to England, several members of the Indian gentry held a meeting at Hooghly express their appreciation of his labours. His humanity, his administrative efficiency, his impartial sense of justice, his concern for the poor, his eagerness to allow local people to decide on local issues without interference from him, his display of total integrity during the indigo disturbances, were all mentioned with a warmth and sincerity that went beyond servile affectation. One letter sent to the meeting summed it all up by referring to Herschel simply as 'Sir William the Good'. Of what turned out to be his biggest claim to fame, however, there was not the slightest mention. Although one of the delegates remarked that 'no trickery, no administrative charlatanism, has for a moment been tolerated under Sir William Herschel, and this intolerance of sham he has made to reach the lowest officials under him', the use of fingerprints to prevent impersonation did not appear on this list. Another alluded to the social events held at Herschel's home (complimenting him on flouting usual practice and inviting 'native gentlemen' as well as Europeans) but although we know that Herschel collected fingerprints from his guests on such occasions, there was no local memory of the magistrate's unusual hobby.

The impact of Herschel's innovation in India was, frankly, minimal. What administrative presence it did have in places like Hooghly dissipated soon after his departure. When, at the request of Francis Galton, he wrote to Bengal in the 1890s, requesting specimens of the fingerprints recorded in the Hooghly registration documents, these were found and sent to him with the eloquent comment that the procedure was no longer used. In 1881, apparently, the Governor of Greenwich Jail in Sydney requested Herschel for a description of his method but seven years later, the baronet declared that he did not know 'what he did thereon'. He himself spent the initial years of his retirement studying theology at Oxford, obtaining a first class in the Honour School of Theology in his late forties ('a course of study at such an age carried through with such thoroughness and eager interest', wrote the Warden of Keble College after Herschel's death, 'is *optimi exempli*') and having been gently persuaded to give up the idea of ordination, lectured at Hertford College for some years on divinity and was active as a philanthropist. Apart from occasionally collecting prints from friends (as he had done for so many years), he did not do a thing to publicize what he and virtually the entire world would later claim as his discovery.

He was shaken out of his torpor in 1880 when *Nature* published a contribution on fingerprint identification from an obscure medical missionary in Tokyo. The career of its author, Henry Faulds, had begun in India in 1872, where he had served at his mission's station in Darjeeling, in northern Bengal.

In less than a year, however, he had fallen out with the missionary heading the station and returned to Scotland, where the Church of Scotland's Foreign Mission Committee terminated his appointment. Faulds got married and joined the United Presbyterian Church of Scotland, whose Foreign Mission Board agreed to send him to Japan, where he arrived in 1874 and set up a hospital and dispensary in 'the foreign concession' adjoining Tokyo. One does not know how energetic he was in spreading the word of Christ but he was certainly an active proselytizer for Western medicine. He introduced Listerian antiseptic principles in Japan, lectured on Darwinism, founded a mini-medical school, and was offered the post of personal physician to a prince at an astronomical salary of £1,000 if he gave up his mission work. He declined. In 1885, he returned to England because of his wife's illness and never returned to Japan.

'Somewhere about 1878', his most vocal admirer later recounted, 'while walking on the beach in the Bay of Yedo in Japan', he stumbled upon some pieces of prehistoric 'sun-baked' pottery bearing 'the finger-impressions of the Japanese potters left on the clay while still soft'. Faulds had never encountered any scientific discussion of fingerprints but he was greatly interested in the physiology of touch and noticed 'the unique patterns which the papillary ridges formed'. After pondering the marks on the pottery for some time, Faulds decided to collect specimens of fingerprints. (It is not impossible that he had encountered the common practice among non-literate Indians of signing with their thumb marks while in Darjeeling. One sees no reason, however, why he should have attributed his insight to Japanese sources if that had indeed been the case.) He had developed a system for noting his observations on cards, each carrying outlines of both hands with 'the lineations filled in with pencil' (a technique he soon gave up in favour of prints of inked fingers) and 'recording nationality, sex, colour of eyes and hair, and securing a specimen of the latter'. (He would later reveal that he had included the lock of hair because he had read in an anthropological paper that hair was one of the best means of identifying race. More than four decades later, he still thought the 'subject might still merit a little attention'.) Beginning in 1878, he sent out these forms with a circular to people all over the world. 'I am at present engaged in a comparative study of the *rugae*, or skin-furrows, of the hands of different races', the circular began. After providing instructions on how to obtain clear prints, Faulds promised 'novel and valuable ethnological results from this enquiry'. The response, however, was disappointing, most choosing to ignore the request.

So, in February 1880, Faulds decided to write a letter to Charles Darwin about the curious marks. Although deeply religious, Faulds held Darwin in the highest regard and described himself in the letter as 'an ardent student of your writings'. After telling Darwin about his discovery of finger-prints on ancient pottery and his investigations of 'the rugae or furrows on the palmar surface of the human hand', he observed, 'the few monkeys etc. which I have got show similar but *somewhat* different markings and if man's origin has been from organised "dust" perhaps a comparative study of lemuroids etc. may yield results of real value – I hope for this and bethought myself of your powerful aid – A word or two would set observers working everywhere'. Faulds's own interest in finger furrows, however, was far more practical – which, the Scotsman remarked to Darwin, should appeal to the English – and his four suggestions on the potential value of the ridges were all concerned with 'identification in medico-legal studies'. Number one was: 'Copies of palmar impressions of convicted criminals – as photographs now are used – the latter become unlike the original, the rugae, never'. Faulds, however, was not concerned with criminology alone. Since he believed that '*heredity rules here* marvellously', he speculated in his letter to Darwin whether in cases like that of the Tichborne claimant, one could reach a decision by ascertaining whether the claimant's 'rugae were of the Tichborne or Orton type'. Still focusing on heredity, he suggested, 'in cases where mutilated remains are found and various people are missing', one could compare the rugae (presumably of the discovered parts of the body) with 'that of the parents etc.' His fourth and final point on the possible practical utility of the rugae was almost an afterthought, and a barely complete one: 'Where impressions exist of bloody fingers by a murderer, or prints on fresh paint or drinking glasses, windows etc. by a robber – Etc.'

In his reply, the author of *The Origin of Species*, then only

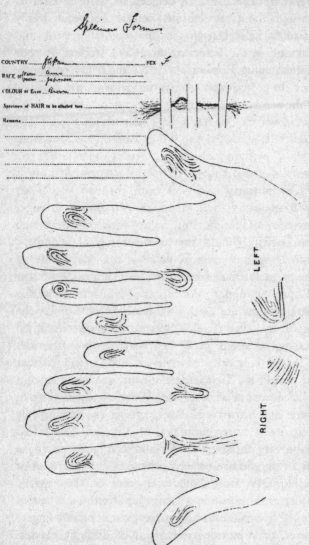

Specimen Forms

COUNTRY ....*Japan*........ SEX *F*

RACE of {Father ....*Ainu*....
         {Mother ...*Japanese*...

COLOUR of Eyes ...*Brown*...

Specimen of HAIR to be attached here ....

Remarks ....

LEFT

RIGHT

FACSIMILE (REDUCED) OF THE ORIGINAL, OUTLINE FORMS FOR BOTH HANDS.
Done in copperplate for the author in Japan at close of 1879 or in January, 1880. The lineations were
filled in with pencil at the same period.

FIGURE 10

Faulds's original fingerprint forms (1880).

two years away from his death, described the topic as 'a curious one' but begged off any personal involvement on account of ill-health. Instead, he said, he had forwarded the letter to 'Mr F Galton, who is the most likely man that I can think of to take up the subject to make further inquiries'. This he did, with this note:

> My Dear Galton,
> The enclosed letter and circular may perhaps interest you, as it relates to a queer subject. You will perhaps say hang his impudence. But seriously the letter might possibly be worth taking some day to the Anthropology Inst. for the chance of someone caring about it.

Francis Galton – Darwin's cousin, pre-eminent scientist, the-orist of heredity and the man who coined the term 'eugenics' – would later play a major role in the establishment of finger-prints in criminal identification. In April 1880, however, he had little interest in the subject. 'I will take Faulds' letter to the Anthro.[pological Institute]', he promised, 'and see what can be done; indeed, I myself got several thumb impressions a couple of years ago, having heard of the Chinese plan with criminals, but failed, probably from want of sufficiently minute obser-vation, to make out any large number of differences . . . Any-how I will do what I can to help Mr. Faulds in getting these sort of facts and in having an extract from his letter printed'. None of those promises was kept.

Faulds, however, was not waiting on Galton. On 28 October 1880, *Nature* published a long letter from him 'on the skin-furrows of the hand'. In it, Faulds described how the marks found on the prehistoric pottery shards had been too 'vague and ill defined' to be of much use, 'but a comparison of such finger-tip impressions made in recent pottery led me to observe the characters of the skin-furrows in human fingers generally'. Later, he added that he had also been drawn to the subject by his interest in the physiology of touch and also because, 'having myopic eyes which enable me to write with ease the Lord's Prayer three times in the space of a sixpence, I soon noticed the unique patterns which the papillary ridges formed'. He also collected 'a large number of nature-prints' from Japanese acquaintances and from 'different nationalities, which I hope may aid students of ethnology in classification'.

'The dominancy of heredity through these infinite varieties', Faulds remarked, 'is sometimes very striking. I have found unique patterns in a parent repeated with marvellous accuracy in his child'. He thought it important to caution, however, that 'negative results . . . might prove nothing in regard to parentage'.

So what was the use of these marks? Apart from their use in ethnology, 'when bloody finger-marks or impressions on clay, glass, &c., exist, they may lead to the scientific identification of criminals'. He himself, Faulds reported, had succeeded in detecting, by the study of greasy thumbprints on the bottle, 'who had been drinking some rectified spirit' at his hospital. 'Other cases', he added, 'might occur in medico-legal investigations, as when the hands only of some mutilated victim were found. If previously known they would be much more precise in value than the standard *mole* of the penny novelists. If unknown previously, heredity might enable an expert to determine the relatives with considerable probability in many cases, and with absolute precision in some'. He concluded with the declaration that 'there can be no doubt as to the advantage of having, besides their photographs, a nature-copy of the for-ever-unchangeable finger-furrows of important criminals'.

Between 1886 and 1888, Faulds spoke to officials in Scotland Yard (especially Inspector John Tunbridge of the CID, whom Faulds called one of Scotland Yard's 'most enlightened officers') about the use of fingerprints for identification. He volunteered 'to work a small bureau, free of expense, in order to test its value and practicability'. Faulds proposed the registration of the prints of all ten fingers and even prepared forms for the purpose. There was no great enthusiasm for his proposal. One official asked, 'How could anyone be convicted on identification of features confined within so small a space as the tip or pad of a finger?' Tunbridge himself may not have been wholly sceptical – although his report to the Commissioner in 1887 was never available to anybody outside the Yard and is believed to be lost, Faulds himself believed that he had praised Faulds's idea as 'scientific and accurate' but 'too delicate for ordinary police manipulation' and also in need of legislative authorization. Later, Tunbridge became Commissioner of Police in New Zealand and introduced the fingerprint system there, writing to Faulds in 1907 that he was puzzled why 'since the F. P. system has been adopted as a means of identification of criminals with such marked success . . . you have not been more actively connected with the carrying out of the system'.

It was the 1880 letter from Faulds that first induced Herschel to reveal his Indian experience with fingerprints to the public. It came as a bolt from the blue to Faulds, who had never read anything by Herschel on the subject – before Faulds's letter to *Nature*, there was not a scrap to be read except for the brief remark to the Indigo Commission – and had never heard of Herschel's work from anybody in India. Nevertheless, Herschel's claim to have been the first to introduce fingerprint identification was endorsed by influential figures in the 1890s, including Francis Galton and the members of the Troup Committee we encountered in Chapter 1. 'After all that has been written', Herschel himself declared at the age of seventy-six in a letter to *The Times*, 'I claim that to myself was first given the idea of fingerprints affording the irresistible proof of identity which it is now notorious that they can be made to yield; also the perception of the simplicity with which their power can be brought to bear on the great bulk of those frauds that corrupt public morality; and so, the conviction of their enormous value to the cause of justice and of truthfulness. Further, that I worked it out from 1858 to 1879, directly in order to satisfy a crying need, amid the depressing difficulties of a Government official in India'. By 1909, however, fingerprints in England had come to be allied firmly to police work and Herschel disavowed any credit for introducing fingerprints in the forensic domain ('I deliberately set that aside as premature') – it was Galton and 'Professor Faulds of Tokio' who, he declared, had first demonstrated that potential.

Faulds, however, was far from appeased by such gestures, let alone by the mistaken promotion to a professorship. Progressively marginalized by the fast-developing fingerprint establishment and its recognized saints, the doctor turned quite nasty. He wrote several books and pamphlets on the subject of fingerprinting and published a short-lived journal on forensic identification called *Dactylography*, in all of which he defended his claim as the true pioneer of fingerprinting in increasingly shrill tones, but to no great effect. He spent his last years in a somewhat peripatetic medical career in England, dying in Stoke on Trent at the age of eighty-six in 1930. By then, fingerprinting had become a cornerstone of police practice in Britain but the name of Faulds was rarely uttered – and never in praise – by its champions. The dazzling new technique had written its own official history, one tailored in significant ways to highlight the contributions of some and ignore those of others. According to this authorized history, three brilliant pioneers established the science and practice of fingerprinting: William James Herschel, Francis Galton and Edward Richard Henry.

Oddly enough, it was Herschel alone who ever gave any sincere credit to Faulds. In 1917, in response to Faulds's furious assault on the relevance of Konai's handprint, Herschel acknowledged that Faulds had indeed been the first to suggest the use of fingerprinting for the identification of criminals – 'for all of which I gave him, and I still do so, the credit due for a conception so different from mine'. This was Herschel's last personal contribution to the fingerprint debate. He was to die that very year – reportedly of a stroke suffered while he was taking his own fingerprints, which he had done more than a hundred times since 1859.

The dispute between Faulds and Herschel over the title of pioneer has occupied far too much space in the history of fingerprinting. The issue, however, is really quite simple to resolve. Faulds had a clearer insight into the *criminological* importance of fingerprints than Herschel and had strong ideas on the persistence of the ridge patterns. But brilliant intuitions, however worthy of applause, are not enough to guarantee lasting recognition. Faulds just could not proffer the voluminous evidence needed to establish his contentions. His work was conceived and conducted in a strictly scientific way – but it was paradoxically weak in the vital raw material of science: evidence. Herschel, on the other hand, had never approached fingerprinting in a scientific spirit. A colonial civil servant driven by suspicions of Indians – and let us not overlook in our postcolonial cynicism a genuine compulsion to ensure impartial and certain justice – Herschel introduced fingerprints simply as an administrative innovation. Even the use of fingerprints to determine racial or hereditary questions – a chimera chased for years by scientists such as Galton and of importance to Faulds – did not really interest him. He once mentioned that the differences between the ridge patterns of Hindus and Europeans were clear but not invariable enough to be used for identification. That was all. The biological significance of the ridge patterns, if any, was not his concern, only their identifying characteristics.

Again paradoxically, it was the wholly unscientific baronet, who, because of his administrative experience with the procedure and because of his extensive personal store of prints collected over years from the same individuals, possessed the evidence essential for establishing the scientific worth of finger-prints as unique and enduring markers of individual identity. Faulds, for instance, had suspected that the ridge patterns persisted unchanged through life. While in Tokyo, he had even tried the experiment of shaving off the ridges with a razor and waiting to see if they grew back in their original form. When they did so, he felt confident that the patterns were 'for-ever-unchangeable'. As Herschel was quick to point out later, the number of experiments conducted by Faulds and their duration simply did not permit him to draw such a definite conclusion. Only his specimens were large enough in number, taken often enough from the same person and at long enough intervals to prove it irrefutably. What remained to be achieved was a systematic and easily searchable system of *classification* of fingerprints, and although Faulds claimed to have evolved such a system, he did not publish any details and failed to attract any police or government interest to it. Herschel, too, had tried to evolve a classification but like most of his work, it had never been published.

Perhaps more importantly, the English elite of the turn of the century operated almost like a club and Faulds possessed neither the social connections nor the social skills essential to enter it. He was as much of an outsider as it was possible to be in the England of his time: a Scotsman who had not been born in the right kind of family, had not been to the right kind of school, did not know the right kind of people, a doctor but far from an eminent one, and by temperament combative, brusque and downright 'ill-bred', to use the terminology of the era. His ordinary origins and his acerbic personality antagonized people such as Galton who might have helped him gain some renown. And Galton was *the* crucial figure in this matter. Even Herschel might have died without much recognition had his work not been discovered by that energetic, prolific polymath. It was Galton who endorsed the scientific value of Herschel's evidence

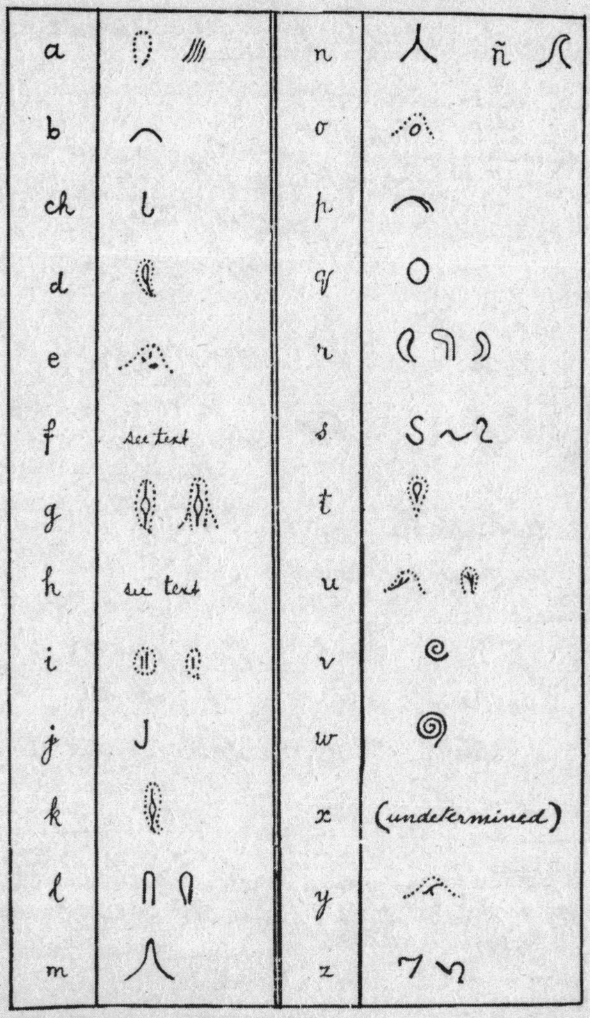

VOWELS AND CONSONANTS IN SYLLABIC CLASSIFICATION
with typical specimens of figure elements.

FIGURE 11

Faulds's proposed classification of fingerprint patterns (1912).

Symbols for Classification

$\mathcal{L}$ r   Loop, right.

$\mathcal{L}$ L   Loop, left

2 $\mathcal{L}$ r   Two loops, right

2 $\mathcal{L}$ L   same left

$\mathcal{L}$ line r   loop line right

$\mathcal{L}$ line L   d°   left

$\mathcal{L}$ sp. N   loop spiral in the direction of the letter N

$\mathcal{L}$ sp U   loop spiral in the direction of the letter U

d $\mathcal{L}$ sp. N

d $\mathcal{L}$ sp U

---

sp. N   Spiral N

sp U   Spiral U

d sp N   double spiral N

d sp U   U

Special combinations of $\mathcal{L}$ & sp

sp N L   Spiral N, L

dsp N L   double spiral N, L

$\mathcal{L}$ sp U

R   Ring

dot R   Dot-ring

Lf r   Leaf right

Lf L   " left

6 lines between the
first true loop lines
A.F. Etheridge. 1.r.
1890.

2 Ys united

Same. 2. r.

Dot & 2 circles
Harriett Mott.
1. r.   1890

Loop~~point dot~~ is really an
end line.
The angular turns are
not sharper than in the
original.
2 r; Revd T. H. Tydd. 1890

Spiral, perfect, with
4 complete, clean
turns & then an 'end'.
1 r.   7. M. Strand 1890

Double Spiral.
2 r. W. Welch. 1890

FIGURE 12

Pages from Herschel's 1890 attempt at classification. His autograph
note reads: 'Classification. The only serious attempt I made –
Classification is entirely Galton's work'.

and disseminated it in influential quarters that were closed to Faulds and which Herschel himself never showed any interest in. But Galton did even more. His account of the history of fingerprinting became the official history of the technique after it was established in Britain and in this, the grateful Galton accorded pride of place to Herschel as the founding father. (When Galton had first approached Herschel for his fingerprint specimens, the baronet had agreed wholeheartedly, insisting, however, that Galton acknowledge his pioneering studies. This Galton did with an energy that blew others, such as Faulds, out of the way.) Nor were Galton's contributions confined to establishing fingerprinting in Britain. Without stirring from London, he was instrumental in revivifying fingerprint identification in India itself and inspiring its further development into a usable police technique. It may not be easy to answer the question 'Who discovered fingerprints?' but there is a simple, unequivocal answer to the question 'Who brought fingerprints to public and official attention in Britain *and* India, stimulating new research leading to the universal adoption of the technique?' It was Francis Galton.

FOUR

'Little Worlds in Themselves'

Francis Galton (1822–1911) was scientist as well as sage, inventor as well as statistical wizard – combinations that could, perhaps, have occurred only in the Victorian era, and not too often even then.

Galton's most familiar legacy, however, is the word 'eugenics'. He not merely coined the term but propounded some of its fundamental concepts, writing extensively and influentially on the nature and importance of inheritance, race and intelligence. For his whole life, Galton laboured to discover whether individuals, although unique at one level, also faithfully represented their types – the *races* to which they belonged. Did individual Jews, in spite of all their differences, still embody common traits characterizing the Jewish Type? To investigate such questions, he came up with his technique of composite photography: if portraits of individuals were superimposed on one another, then, he argued, the final result would cancel out the differences and show only the common features, the traits of the type that the individuals belonged to.

Galton was tireless in collecting data that could shed light on heredity and after a partially successful attempt to obtain information from the public about their physical traits, personal aptitudes and family histories through a prize offer, he was inspired to design and operate an anthropometric laboratory at the South Kensington International Health Exhibition in 1884.

FIGURE 13
Francis Galton.

This was an area of 6 feet by 36 feet, crammed with instruments of his own design, where visitors to the exhibition could have themselves measured and tested by Galton or his assistants for the price of three pennies. The data recorded were wide-ranging: weight and height, of course, but also the length of limbs, the strength of pull, force of blow, keenness of hearing, and colour discrimination. At the end of the examination, the visitor was handed a card containing all his data and Galton kept a copy for his own file. About ten thousand people visited the laboratory and, when the Health Exhibition closed in 1885, Galton moved it to what is now the Science Museum, where it remained open for almost eight years. It was Galton's hope that the measurements compiled there would yield conclusive information about how bodily dimensions were correlated with one another 'as between the length of different limbs, between stature and strength, weight and lung capacity, and very many other related measures'. Questions of heredity, as always, were also on Galton's mind: he soon invited visitors to answer 'a brief list of questions, both personal and family . . . one of them is whether the parents were first cousins'.

Since Galton was interested not simply in racial characteristics but also in the ways that the individual human being's unique attributes might reveal clues to hereditary and racial influences, he was greatly interested in techniques of identification. Often, Galton would even forget about race and inheritance, concentrating on the peculiarities of each individual that could be used to identify him. For example, he was intrigued by Bertillon's anthropometric methods – which could be applied to racial biology but never were by Bertillon – and visited him in 1888, when he had had his mugshot taken and, 'greatly impressed by the celerity and apparent sureness of the work', wondered whether 'this application of anthropometry to rogues' could 'also be of service to honest men'.

There was the inevitable allusion to the Tichborne affair and

FIGURE 14

Bertillon's mugshot of Galton, 1893.

'the enormous waste of money, effort, and anxiety which might have been spared, had Roger Tichborne passed through an anthropometric laboratory before he went abroad'. It was simple indeed to prevent such a contretemps – all that was needed was 'for every person about to leave his country for a long time, having regard to the various accidents of good or ill-fortune, to be properly measured, and to leave a copy of his measurements in the safe keeping of an anthropometric laboratory'. On his return from Paris, the Royal Institution asked him to lecture on the subject and it was while drafting this lecture that he decided to investigate whether it was true, as he had heard, that fingerprints could also be used to identify individuals. (He never disclosed his initial sources but the letter forwarded by Darwin from Faulds was the likeliest candidate.) He wrote to the editor of *Nature*, asking for information. The letter was never published but the editor put him in touch with William James Herschel. Thus began a long and mutually stimulative collaboration leading to far-reaching consequences.

As soon as Galton had taken a look at some of the specimen prints sent to him by Herschel, his interest in Bertillonage began to wane. The ridges on the fingertips, Galton decided, were 'by far the most permanent of all external human peculiarities and the surest known means of personal identification'. Visitors to his anthropometric laboratory were now asked for their thumb impressions in addition to measurements and other physical data. One reason why Galton persisted for so long with his Anthropometric Laboratory was, in fact, because it offered him a great opportunity to collect fingerprints. The Laboratory was a popular attraction – celebrities dropped in frequently. A famous story recounts (apocryphally) how, after measuring the immense head of Mr Gladstone, the Grand Old Man of British politics, Galton informed him that the only head bigger was Galton's own. Herschel visited the laboratory twice and treasured his measurement cards in his collection of papers and fingerprints.

Galton's faith in fingerprint identification developed in leaps and bounds: he was soon deprecating the Bertillon system in the pages of *Nature* for being too cumbersome and imprecise on its own. He then prodded Bertillon himself into including fingerprints on his anthropometric cards, although, as we have seen, the Frenchman continued to use the measurements to file the cards. Galton was perfectly comfortable with this: fingerprints alone could not, as yet, be used to classify thousands of records. But finger marks were nonpareil 'for final identification', he declared, adding that they provided 'the only means of surely identifying growing youths' whose measurements would change over the years.

Galton's 1892 book, *Finger Prints*, was his last major technical work but his first step toward the most enduring contribution to British public life that he was ever to make. For all his hopes about eugenics, for all the popularity of eugenic measures in various nations, and for all the effect that popularity had on the lives of particular groups, eugenics, fortunately, never became a fundamental feature of British administrative practice. Fingerprinting, in contrast, became an indispensable part of policing in Britain long before Galton died and it is questionable whether, without his efforts in assembling the different fragments of knowledge and evidence on the subject and circulating this complete version with his formidable scientific imprimatur within his immense circle of influence, the fingerprint revolution could have occurred quite as quickly as it did. The history of fingerprinting is a complex web but at its centre sits Francis Galton, with all the major strands meeting in him and passing through him.

His biographer relates that Galton later regretted the time and energy he had expended on the subject of fingerprints but there is no sign of that regret in his 1892 book, which heaves with the joy of discovery. Every page is littered with evidence of the painstaking, exhaustive, almost obsessive research that

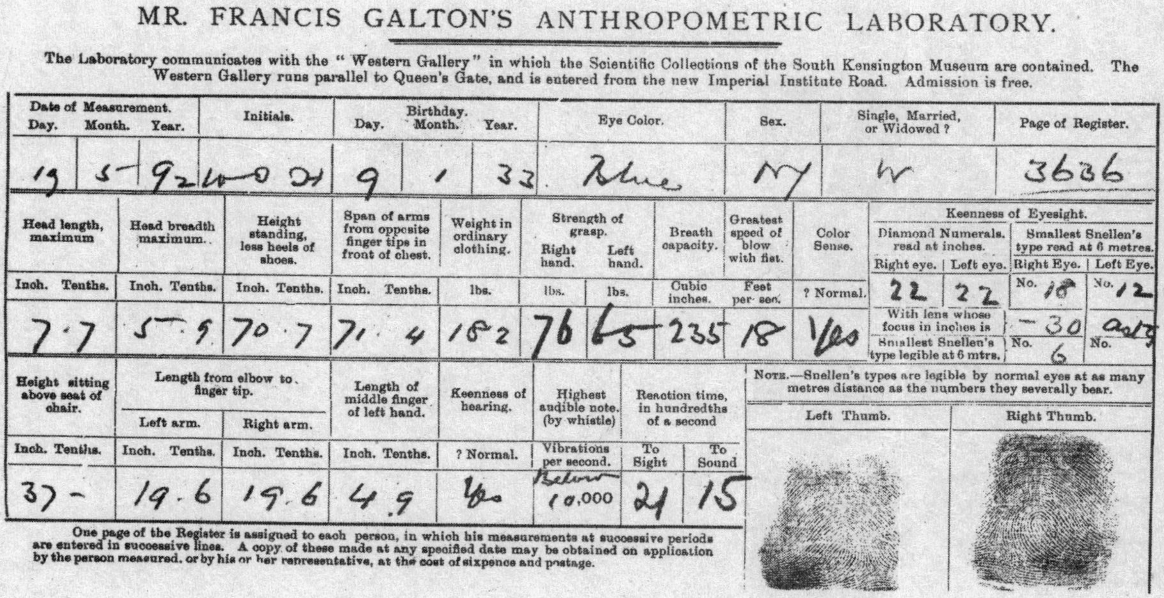

MR. FRANCIS GALTON'S ANTHROPOMETRIC LABORATORY.

The Laboratory communicates with the "Western Gallery" in which the Scientific Collections of the South Kensington Museum are contained. The Western Gallery runs parallel to Queen's Gate, and is entered from the new Imperial Institute Road. Admission is free.

Date of Measurement. Day.	Month.	Year.	Initials.	Birthday. Day.	Month.	Year.	Eye Color.	Sex.	Single, Married, or Widowed?	Page of Register.
19	5	92	[illegible]	9	1	33	Blue	M	W	3636

Head length, maximum	Head breadth maximum.	Height standing, less heels of shoes.	Span of arms from opposite finger tips in front of chest.	Weight in ordinary clothing.	Strength of grasp. Right hand.	Left hand.	Breath capacity.	Greatest speed of blow with fist.	Color Sense.	Keenness of Eyesight. Diamond Numerals, read at inches. Right eye.	Left eye.	Smallest Snellen's type read at 6 metres. Right Eye.	Left Eye.
Inch. Tenths.	Inch. Tenths.	Inch. Tenths.	Inch. Tenths.	lbs.	lbs.	lbs.	Cubic inches.	Feet per sec.	? Normal.				
7.7	5.9	70.7	71.4	182	76	65	235	18	Yes	22	22	No. 18	No. 12
										With lens whose focus in inches is		-30	[illegible]
										Smallest Snellen's type legible at 6 mtrs.		No. 6	No.

Height sitting above seat of chair.	Length from elbow to finger tip. Left arm.	Right arm.	Length of middle finger of left hand.	Keenness of hearing.	Highest audible note. (by whistle)	Reaction time, in hundredths of a second. To Sight	To Sound
Inch. Tenths.	Inch. Tenths.	Inch. Tenths.	Inch. Tenths.	? Normal.	Vibrations per second.		
37 –	19.6	19.6	4.9	Yes	Below 10,000	21	15

NOTE.—Snellen's types are legible by normal eyes at as many metres distance as the numbers they severally bear.

Left Thumb. Right Thumb.

One page of the Register is assigned to each person, in which his measurements at successive periods are entered in successive lines. A copy of these made at any specified date may be obtained on application by the person measured, or by his or her representative, at the cost of sixpence and postage.

FIGURE 15

William James Herschel's anthropometric data, recorded by Francis Galton, 1892.

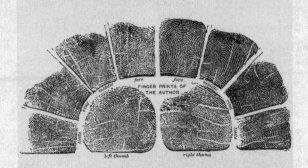

FINGER PRINTS

BY

FRANCIS GALTON, F.R.S., ETC.

London

MACMILLAN AND CO.

AND NEW YORK

1892

All rights reserved

FIGURE 16

Galton's own fingerprints printed on the title page
of his magnum opus.

he had conducted on those extraordinary ridges, the value of which, he averred, would surely have been appreciated earlier if only they had been bigger. 'Had Dean Swift', he mused, 'known and thought of them when writing about the Brobdingnags, whom he constructs on a scale twelve times as great as our own, he would certainly have made Gulliver express horror at the ribbed fingers of the giants who handled him'.

The whole palm was covered with systems of ridges but it was 'the small independent systems which appear on the bulbs of the thumb and fingers' that were the most important. (Of least importance were the three major creases on the palm which engrossed palmists.) The feet and toes, too, possessed their distinctive ridges but being less complex than those of the fingertips, they were best ignored. Studies of aborted foetuses had established that the ridges appeared in the human embryo as early as in the fourth month and they were fully formed by the sixth month. As the individual grew, so did the ridges, remaining distinct 'until old age has set in, when an incipient disintegration of the texture of the skin spoils, and may largely obliterate them'. They were most distinct in the hands of those who did a moderate amount of manual work, being 'but faintly developed in the hands of ladies, rendered delicate by the continual use of gloves and lack of manual labour, and in idiots of the lowest type who are incapable of labouring at all'. The surface of the ridges was punctuated by openings of sweat ducts, which, too, were visible in imprints and could help in identification.

But was all this study of fingerprints worthwhile if the patterns changed over the years? Before fingerprints could be accepted as the basis of identification, it had to be proved that the ridge patterns were permanent features of the body. Galton's energy in collecting and analysing fingerprints was virtually unparalleled – the Galton papers at University College London hold box after large box crammed with fingerprint specimens and correspondence related to them – but this collection was too new to contain prints taken from the same individuals across many years. Without such samples, Galton could not argue that the passage of years did not change the patterns, and without that crucial evidence, his enterprise was unlikely to impress experts on criminal identification. Where, then, could he find such a collection assembled over many years?

His saviour was Herschel. Herschel may have given up his early hopes of bringing about an administrative revolution with fingerprints but he had retained all the prints he had collected over decades. Since even Faulds had not begun investigating fingerprints as early as he had, Herschel alone possessed the unassailable evidence of the permanence of ridge patterns. He offered Galton his unstinted assistance, stipulating only that 'the fact of my having had it in full official practice in India in 1877 after nearly twenty years experimenting, should be recognized'. (The American writer Colin Beavan has recently portrayed this as a secret pact to exclude Faulds's claim. Since Faulds could not really claim to have demonstrated the lifelong persistence of patterns as thoroughly as Herschel, Beavan's conspiracy theory is entirely inaccurate.)

Herschel began by sending Galton imprints of his own fingertips, made in 1860, 1874, 1883 and 1888. On comparing the 1860 and 1888 prints, Galton found 'an obvious amount of wearing and of coarseness' in the latter due to ageing but the essential pattern of the ridges had not changed. This was exactly the kind of evidence of lifelong persistence that was required – but one item, although of great interest, was not sufficient. 'It would be well worth while to hunt up and take the present finger prints of such of the Hindoos as may now be alive, whose impressions were taken in India by Sir W. J. Herschel and still preserved', Galton commented in *Finger Prints*. 'Many years must elapse before my own large collection of finger prints will be available for the purpose of testing persistence during long periods'.

Prodded by Galton, the ever-obliging baronet reactivated his old connections in India, writing to his former assistant Henry Cotton, now the Chief Secretary of the Government of Bengal, asking him to send about eight or ten of the fingerprints from an old register of deeds at Hooghly along with new prints taken from those same individuals. 'The Registration Dept', he recalled, 'had most; so did the Jail, but it may be difficult to find ex-prisoners as easily'. He finally added: 'I shall be glad indeed to know whether the system fell through on my departure, or survived at all'. The Joint Magistrate of Hooghly, F. W. Duke, reported that 'although the practice [of taking finger impressions on deeds] has been discontinued, the register for 1878 has been preserved'. From this register, names were selected of people who lived nearby and were still alive – 'After fourteen years', Mr Duke grumbled, 'the range of selection amongst persons still living and reasonably accessible is very limited' – and the Special Sub-Registrar was sent to visit them and collect fresh prints separately as well as next to the originals. 'The impressions', the Joint Magistrate reported, 'are far from perfect but most of them are sufficiently clear to afford striking evidence of persistence not only of the general character but some of the individual lines'.

Examining these, Galton was at last satisfied that although the 'proportions of the patterns' changed as the shape of the finger changed due to ageing, disease or deformity, the directions and convolutions of the ridges were practically immutable. Just as a pattern on lace would look different but remain fundamentally unaltered if the lace were to be crumpled, the dimensions of a fingerprint would reflect changes in the shape of the finger but the direction or consistency of the lines of the pattern would not be affected. This permanence, Galton emphasized, was virtually unique:

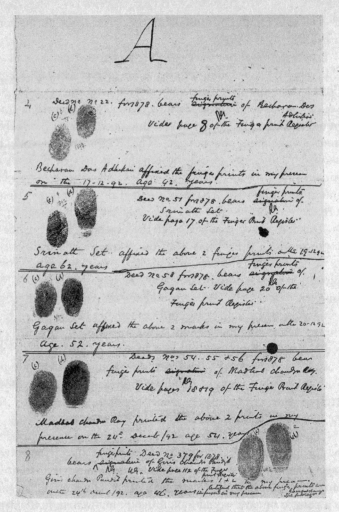

FIGURE 17

More evidence of pattern persistence: fresh (1892) prints
from some Hooghly residents who had signed deeds with their
fingerprints in 1878. Collected by local authorities at the
request of Herschel, who had been prompted by Galton.

There appear to be no means of personal identification other than deep scars and tattoo marks, comparable in their permanence and certainty with those of the thumb and finger marks. All the dimensions of the limb alter in the slow course of growth and decay. The colour of the hair, the quality and tint of the skin, the expression of the features, the gestures, the handwriting, even the eye colour, change after many years. There seems to be no persistence anywhere in the bodily structure, except in these minute and too much disregarded papillary ridges.

Fingerprints, in short, were enduring as well as unique and, therefore, ideal markers of the identity of the individual. Statistical investigations had convinced Galton that the chance that two identical fingerprints were made by different individuals was less than '1 in about sixty-four thousand millions'. When prints from two different fingers matched two prints from separate fingers, it was virtually impossible that they could be from two different people. 'We read', Galton concluded, 'of the dead body of Jezebel being devoured by the dogs of Jezreel . . . and that the dogs left only her skull, the palms of her hands, and the soles of her feet; but the palms of the hands and the soles of the feet are the very remains by which a corpse might be most surely identified, if impressions of them, made during life, were available'.

Galton recommended the use of fingerprinting as a sure means of identification for anybody at risk of misidentification. 'Is this criminal an old offender? Is this new recruit a deserter? Is this professed pensioner personating a man who is dead? Is this upstart claimant to property the true heir, who was believed to have died in foreign lands?' In most cases requiring the identification of a criminal, the question usually boiled down to 'Who is this unknown person X? Is his name contained in such and such a register?' So far, systematic criminal registers were maintained only within the Bertillon system but the complex

UNIVERSITY OF WINCHESTER LIBRARY

series of measurements offered many an opportunity for error and it wasn't even certain that all of Bertillon's measurements were independent variables. (If a measure varied in correlation with another, then it was not of great value in identification, and could be omitted.) Fingerprints, however, differed quite independently, apparently without relation to any known biological factor: 'It would be totally impossible to fail to distinguish between the finger prints of twins, who in other respects are exactly alike'. The inclusion of fingerprints in the Bertillon system would, therefore, 'increase its power fully five-hundred fold'. (And this, of course, is what Bertillon himself soon did, on Galton's advice.) Secondly, if the fingerprints on record agreed with the fingerprints of a suspect, that evidence of identity 'vastly exceeds all that can be derived from any number of ordinary anthropometric data. *By itself it is amply sufficient to convict.* Bertillonage can rarely supply more than grounds for very strong suspicion: the method of finger prints affords certainty'. The 'two great and peculiar merits of finger prints' were that they were 'self-signatures, free from all possibility of faults in observation or of clerical error; and they apply throughout life'.

Fingerprints, then, were permanent identifiers. But if they were to be used on a large scale for identification, say, of criminals, then one would need to compile a register of prints which would be searched for a matching print. In order for a register like that to be searchable, the immense multitude of patterns would need to be sorted into coherent, well-demarcated groups. And this was where Galton faced his greatest challenge. Herschel, as we have seen, had evolved a rough and ready system of his own but something far more precise was needed. Gradually, Galton learnt to divide the patterns into three basic categories of arches, loops and whorls, with loops being the commonest variety. (In his 1880 letter in *Nature*, Faulds had used the terms 'loop' and 'whorl' but had not offered any kind of classificatory system, whether based on them or on any other characteristics.)

Things, however, were not always so simple: numerous transitional forms existed linking the arches with the loops, the loops with the whorls, and the arches with the whorls. Any classificatory scheme would have to differentiate these 'compound' or 'composite' patterns but if a scheme had too many categories within it, then it would be difficult to search. These two needs, it seemed, simply could not be reconciled. So difficult was it to assign transitional patterns to any one particular category that Galton's decisions to put a mixed pattern in one group or another did not always match the choices of his own assistant and he finally decided to keep 'his work, in which I have perfect confidence, independent from my own'.

He tried to resolve the issue in different ways but failed to establish any general rule that could be followed in a large set of prints and still enable the set to be searched quickly. Galton, therefore, was forced to concede that the value of fingerprints was probably secondary 'for aid in searching the registers of a criminal intelligence bureau . . . the primary being some form of the already established Bertillon anthropometric method'. He added, however, that 'whatever power the latter gives of successfully searching registers, that power would be multiplied many hundredfold by the inclusion of finger prints, because their peculiarities are entirely unconnected with other personal characteristics . . . besides this, while measurements and photographs are serviceable only for adults, and even then under restrictions, the finger prints are available throughout life'. Fingerprints, in other words, were powerful tools but unusable on their own. Bertillon's measurements might be less dependable and more cumbersome to record but thanks to his superb system of classification, the records could be searched swiftly and the relevant card extracted without confusion, as long as there were no serious discrepancies between the current measurements of

ARCHES.

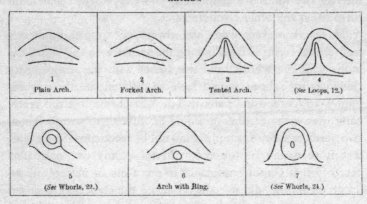

LOOPS.

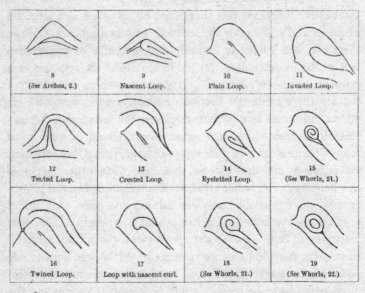

FIGURE 18

The three chief fingerprint patterns: arches, loops and whorls.

the individual being investigated and measurements of the same person that might be on file. Fingerprints, although simpler to record and more distinctive than measurements, were, so far, almost impossible to classify in such a register.

Even in the absence of such a classified register, fingerprints could, Galton argued, be used for certain kinds of identification. They would be especially valuable, Galton emphasized, in 'identifying persons of other races' in the colonies. 'The natives are mostly unable to sign; their features are not readily distinguished by Europeans; and in too many cases they are characterised by a strange amount of litigiousness, wiliness and unveracity'. (Herschel, who had spent his life with 'natives', had never remarked on their physical indistinguishability but Galton and some of his colonial informants made much of this traditional

WHORLS.

20 Small Spiral in Loop.	21 Spiral in Loop.	22 Circlet in Loop.	23 Ring in Loop.
24 Rings.	25 Ellipses.	26 Spiro-rings.	
27 Simple Spiral.	28 Nascent Duplex Spiral.	29 Duplex Spiral.	30 Banded Duplex Spiral.

point.) In his ideas on applying fingerprinting in the colonies, Galton, in fact, was influenced less by Herschel than by one Major Ferris of the Indian Staff Corps, who had spent twenty-three years in India and had recently visited Galton's laboratory. So struck was Galton by Ferris's opinions that he reproduced them at length in his *Finger Prints*. Ferris's first problem in identifying Indians was that 'the colour of hair, eyes and complexion' differed little, as did their hand-writing, which, regardless of script, was 'devoid of character'.

Secondly, Indians were obsessed with preserving and adding to their ancestral landholdings to a degree that 'passes the comprehension of the ordinary Western mind'. This 'passion, or religion, coupled with a natural taste for litigation' resulted in an enormous number of civil suits over disputed titles. Allegations of fraudulent transfers of land were frequent and since the majority of landholders were illiterate, documentary fraud was only too common. For instance, Ferris reported, every British administrator in India was familiar with repudiations of transfer of title, 'the person purporting to have executed the transfer asserting that he had no knowledge of it, and never authorised any one to write, sign, or present it for registration'. Ferris was unwilling to go too deeply into 'the ethics of falsehood among Western and Eastern peoples', merely stressing that what Westerners might consider 'downright lying' seemed to an Indian to be 'no more than venial prevarication'. Hence, perjury was rampant in Indian courts 'to an extent unknown in the United Kingdom'. (As Galton himself was to opine later, 'while the natives of India and of Egypt have beautiful traits of character and some virtues in an exceptional degree, their warmest admirers would not rank veracity among them . . . if a map of the world were tinted with gradations of colour to show the percentage of false testimony in courts of law . . . England would be tinted rather lightly and both Bengal and Egypt very darkly'.)

Galton and Ferris, of course, were entirely orthodox in their low opinion of Eastern integrity: no colonialist, not even the far more polite Herschel, would have disagreed with them. The conviction that Indians, in particular, lied as a matter of course and thought nothing of perjuring themselves was well-nigh universal and as with Herschel's whim to ask Rajyadhar Konai for his palm print, the belief led quite naturally to the conviction that fingerprinting might be the weapon against the rampant dishonesty of the 'natives'. It was true, Ferris agreed, that all documents related to land transfer had to be registered but the registration process was far from foolproof, especially when legal loopholes were used to complete it in the absence of the executor. It would, therefore, be a boon if 'some simple but efficient means could be contrived to identify the person who has executed a bond' and the registration law could insist that all documents 'bear the imprint of one or more fingers of the parties to the deed ... In the majority of cases, the mere question would be, Is the man A the same person as B, or is he not? And of that question the finger marks would give unerring proof'. The use of finger marks would also detect fraudulent claimants to pensions.

All of these, of course, were old Herschelian themes, although the racial explanations for Indian 'unveracity' were greatly expanded by Ferris and Galton. It was not just in India where fingerprinting might be useful. The identification of the Chinese, Galton pointed out, was even more difficult than of Indians and he mentioned Taber's efforts to apply finger-printing to the problem. Citing a report from the *British North Borneo Herald* on the 'great difficulty of identifying coolies, either by their photographs or measurements', Galton remarked that fingerprinting might resolve this difficulty.

Meanwhile, more and more people had been worrying about the identification of criminals at home – as we have seen, the Council of the British Association for the Advancement of

Science wrote in 1892 to the Secretaries of State in charge of some of the most important departments of the British government that 'considering the urgent need for a better system of identification than is now in use in the United Kingdom and its dependencies . . . the anthropometric methods in use in France and elsewhere deserve serious inquiry, as to their efficiency, the cost of their maintenance, their general utility, and the propriety of introducing them'. Galton himself had written to *The Times* in 1894, spelling out the benefits of the anthropometric system in combination with fingerprinting. That, of course, was the year that the Troup Committee was set up by the Home Secretary to recommend the best method for identifying habitual criminals and Galton, as we know, was one of its star witnesses, demonstrating to the Committee how simple it was to record fingerprints and how infallible they were in proving identity. The Committee approached no other expert on the topic – although Faulds once met the Chairman, his views do not seem to have made any impression on Troup. 'Finger prints', the Committee declared, 'are an absolute impression taken from the body itself; if a print be taken at all it must necessarily be correct'. (In 1923, an American jurist would go even further, hailing a man's fingerprints as not simply 'testimony about his body, but his body itself'.) For ease of obtaining and for providing *proof* of identity, fingerprints could not be bettered. Indeed, the report declared that the members 'would have been glad if, going beyond Mr. Galton's own suggestion, they could have adopted his system as the sole basis of identification'.

That, however, was prevented by the 'serious difficulties' of applying Galton's method of classification to large collections of prints, as a Criminal Register would undoubtedly be. In a collection of 25,000 imprints, for example, Galton's classification would put 1,500 prints in one category, 'while there would be several other classes each containing between 500 and 1000 imprints'. These were simply too large for practical use. Galton showed them his method of subdividing the largest categories but the Committee found it 'very elaborate, and in the matter of counting of the number of ridges in the loops . . . open to some uncertainty'. Consequently, the Bertillon system was recommended for classification of the records, with final proof of identity coming from fingerprints, which were to be recorded along with the measurements. This combined system, the Committee was convinced, would 'render a wrong identification practically impossible'. Until an easy and rational system of organizing fingerprints came along, there was, indeed, no better option.

It was a major victory for Galton to convince the government that fingerprints, whatever the problems with their classification in a register, were unbeatable in providing proof of identity. In the history of fingerprinting in Britain, nobody preached the gospel more devotedly or more influentially than him. Apart from impressing Charles Troup's committee, he wrote three monographs on fingerprints, sent letters to newspapers and churned out popular articles that acquainted administrators, scientists and large sections of the British public with fingerprints to an unprecedented extent. In the process, he also established the 'official' history of fingerprinting. (To call it official is not, of course, to imply that it is totally wrong. Indeed, it is surprisingly accurate, even though unfair to some, most notably Faulds.) Summarizing whatever was known about the use of finger marks as signatures in pre-modern times, Galton dismissed such traditions as expressions of the 'superstitious' belief that 'personal contact communicates some mysterious essence from the thing touched to the person who touches it'. His work, on the other hand, sought to establish that finger marks, 'when they are properly made . . . are incomparably the most sure and unchanging of all forms of signature'. The lineage of this technique was a short one and apart from Purkyne, Galton hailed the engraver Thomas Bewick as 'the first well-known person who appears to have studied the lineations of the ridges as a means of identification'. Among others who had preceded Galton was 'Mr Fauld [sic], who seems to have taken much pains, and . . . Mr Tabor [sic], the eminent photographer of San Francisco'.

These, however, were, at best, sporadic and more or less blurred visions of the truth; none was even remotely 'comparable in importance to the regular and official employment made of finger prints by Sir William Herschel, during more than a quarter of a century in Bengal', who, Galton emphasized, was 'the first who devised a feasible method for regular use, and afterwards officially adopted it'. Galton was so fulsome toward Herschel that Faulds once taunted him for serving 'as a kind of graceful chorus to Sir William'. In spite of this public statement, in private Faulds had once been somewhat more polite. After the publication of Galton's *Finger Prints*, he wrote to Galton, describing the book as a 'lucid and masterly exposition of the subject', which he had 'lent to all our Sergeants and Inspectors in this District [Faulds was then police surgeon in Fenton, Staffordshire] and they have been much interested'. Galton, too, seems to have offered some kind of olive branch, by asking Faulds to share some of his fingerprint material, a request that was declined politely. Galton did not forgive. When Faulds published his *Guide to Finger-Print Identification* in 1905, he damned it and its author in the pages of *Nature*: 'Dr. Faulds . . . overstates the value of his own work, belittles that of others, and carps at evidence recently given in criminal cases . . . it contains nothing new that is of value . . . and much of what Dr. Faulds seems to consider new has long since been forestalled'.

It was Herschel and Herschel alone whom Galton would proclaim to be the progenitor of fingerprint identification – not an unjustifiable choice by any means, but one reinforced, no doubt, by Galton's fondness for titled and talented families. As Galton's biographer D. W. Forrest asserts, 'Herschel was the perfect example of the kind of person Galton was liable to overestimate. If a choice had to be made between the relative achievements of Faulds and Herschel, there could be little doubt in Galton's mind to whom the credit should be given'.

Above all, however, Francis Galton served as a centre of synthesis as well as a source of influence. It was Faulds whose letter to *Nature* had compelled Herschel to make his first public claim to have been the pioneer but it was Galton who was responsible for resurrecting and publishing actual, concrete evidence of Herschel's all-but-forgotten work. It is not too much to say that it was Galton who opened Herschel's eyes to the epochal significance of his work, inducing the baronet to make fresh, more successful efforts on its behalf. Galton and Herschel were a symbiotic pair: but for Galton, we might never have heard of Herschel and but for Herschel, Galton's work on fingerprints might not have had any of the impact it did. Without ever setting foot on Indian soil, Galton not only collected specimens from India that he needed for his own work but eventually brought about the rediscovery and efflorescence of Herschel's innovation in India itself.

But Herschel was not the only figure in this story who was influenced by Galton. We have already heard how Galton persuaded Alphonse Bertillon to add fingerprints to anthropometric cards but this success was a small one compared to what he was to achieve with Edward Henry. It was Galton's 1892 book, *Finger Prints*, and then the master's personal acquaintance that pushed Henry away from Bertillonage and toward fingerprinting with the revolutionary consequences that we shall read about in the next chapter. It was entirely typical of stay-at-home British scientists of the time to collect information on, for example, natural history from acquaintances amongst doctors, military men or administrators serving in India. Joseph Banks, Charles Darwin and geologist Charles Lyell all did so with enthusiasm. But Galton surpassed them all. He did not just collect data through his colonial informants; he stimulated them into new research leading to new, enormous triumphs. Galton's worshipful biographer Karl Pearson (the first Francis Galton Professor of Eugenics at University College London) went so far as to declare that 'if a name is to be given to the system of finger-print identification in the same manner that bertillonage was attached to the anthropometric measurement, then the right term is undoubtedly galtonage'.

Nevertheless, Galton's encounter with fingerprints was, at another level, a story of failures. He fervently hoped that fingerprints might unlock some of the secrets of race and heredity, issues that were, arguably, far closer to his heart than personal identification. It was conceivable that the ridge patterns reflected the deeper structure of the organism and might provide much more than a mere means of identification. These modest furrows might bear 'undeniable evidence' of an individual's 'parentage and near kinships', serve to illuminate 'some of the most interesting biological questions of the day, such as heredity, symmetry, correlation, and the nature of genera and species' and indicate the individual's potential (intelligence, for example) and liabilities (to disease or criminality, for instance). It was clear that in their variety, their individuality, and their potential uses, fingerprints were 'little worlds in themselves' – 'in some respects the most important of all anthropological data'.

To his profound disappointment, however, Galton could not find any statistical correlation between the racial origin of the subject and fingerprints: 'there is no *peculiar* pattern which . . . when met with enables us to assert, or even to suspect, the nationality of the person on whom it appeared'. Nor did the fingerprints of artists differ systematically from those of scientists, and 'prints of eminent thinkers and of eminent statesmen . . . can be matched by those of congenital idiots'. The 'great expectations' with which he had begun his study of fingerprints, he was compelled to admit, had 'been falsified, namely their use in indicating Race and Temperament. I thought that any hereditary peculiarities would almost of necessity vary in different races, and that so fundamental and enduring a feature as the finger markings must in some way be correlated with temperament'. Having examined many English, Welsh, Jewish, black, and Basque prints, he could only find one consistent difference: Jews had more whorled patterns. 'It is doubtful at present', he concluded with palpable chagrin, 'whether it is worth while to pursue the subject, except in the case of the Hill tribes of India . . . for the chance of discovering some characteristic and perhaps a more monkey-like pattern'.

He did not, however, give up. As late as 1903, he embarked upon another massive collection of fingerprints, with the aim of evolving a 'natural classification' of the patterns and applying that scheme to 'a revised study of certain problems which were imperfectly discussed in the concluding chapters of my book *Finger Prints* . . . entitled "Heredity", "Races and Classes" and "Genera" '. He even offered the loan of a portable fingerprinting apparatus and books of forms to those willing to help him. But to no avail. Fingerprints seemed to be unmarked by race and heredity. Nor could Galton find any correlation between the patterns 'and any of the bodily faculties or characteristics. It would be absurd therefore to assert that in the struggle for existence, a person with, say, a loop on his right middle finger has a better chance of survival, or a better chance of early marriage, than one with an arch. Consequently genera and species are here seen to be formed without the slightest aid from either Natural or Sexual Selection'. Since they were exempt from any kind of selection, the different patterns should, through interbreeding, have blended into one. 'But that', observed the puzzled Galton, 'is most assuredly not the case; they refuse to blend . . . Each of the patterns keeps as pure and distinct from the others as if they had been severally descended from a thorough-bred ancestry, each in respect to its own peculiar form'.

Fingerprint identification, on the other hand, brought him extraordinary success. But even here, it was not entirely a victorious tale. Galton never considered personal identification by fingerprinting to be of criminological significance alone. In his approach to fingerprint identification, he followed the imperial path – which was logical since his early research was influenced so deeply by Herschel. As Karl Pearson emphasized, it is clear from everything Galton wrote on the subject that 'he did not think finger-prints were useful solely as a matter of criminal identification'. True, England was not as illiterate a country as India, but even at home, Galton advocated a wide range of applications for fingerprinting that reminds one more of Herschel than of the future Scotland Yard Fingerprint Bureau. People saving money at the Post Office savings bank, Galton suggested, should be asked to record their finger impressions in the deposit book 'and that these should be used as a means of identification, when the depositor sought to draw money from a post-office where he was not known'. It was so easy to learn the rudiments of matching fingerprints that 'it might well be part of the training of many minor civil servants, postmasters, Public Trustee employees, War Office and Admiralty pension-officers, and many other similar officials'. Agreeing with his mentor and hero that fingerprints were supremely qualified for use in land-registration offices and to authenticate personal belongings, bonds and passports, Pearson regretted that there was no central fingerprint registry in England for ordinary people where any individual 'could be registered, and . . . be certain of identification for legal purposes at any time during his life, and for some time after his death'. In an interview with *Cassell's Saturday Journal* in 1896, Galton himself had observed:

> You remember what a stir there was when the rumour spread of a plot to kidnap the Duke of York's baby. Think of all the

national difficulties that would have arisen had he been lost and then professed to be found, but his identity doubted. Many people urged me at the time to propose that his finger-prints should be taken, but I hesitated to move seriously in the matter.

For Galton, the irony was that as far as fingerprinting was concerned, the Empire was far more advanced and adventurous than the mother country. What he did not appreciate was that the British public and its political leaders considered universal identification of ordinary people to be repugnant: the individual's right to live and die unobserved by a bureaucracy was a sacred principle of English liberty. Consequently, it was only in the Empire – to the heathen, subject population of which such a sacred principle did not, of course, apply – that fingerprinting came into relatively general use. In the mother country, the only population of any size that came under its purview was the criminal population, and, in the early days, only that part of it which was considered to be so hardened and dehumanized as to be quite beyond redemption. All of Galton's successes in popularizing fingerprinting as a means of identification were confined to criminal identification, an area that he considered important, but no more important than others. And the longer fingerprinting was used in criminal contexts, the less acceptable it seemed for other uses. Karl Pearson lamented that 'it is almost a catastrophe that the process of finger-printing should have become tainted in the popular mind by a criminal atmosphere'.

More than anybody else, it was Galton who brought finger-printing home from the Empire, but although he himself had an expansive, imperial vision of the potential of fingerprinting, he could not persuade his nation to share that vision. His share of the credit for the transfer of fingerprinting from India was immense; immense, too, must have been his disappointment that the exotic import failed to thrive as luxuriantly in home soil as he had hoped.

FIVE

Meanwhile, Back in the Empire ...

When fingerprinting began in British India with Herschel's small-scale effort, the mark of a finger was simply a signature, albeit not as simple as ancient Chinese finger-dabs might have been. The fingerprints on Herschel's registration forms, for instance, could be matched, years later, with prints taken from the same individuals, showing the persistence of their unique patterns. This, indeed, was a 'signature of exceeding simplicity which it is all but impossible to deny'. This approach, however, could not be applied to the identification of prints from *unknown* individuals, which could only be achieved if unidentified prints could be compared, quickly and reliably, with already identified prints. Our early acquaintance, Harry Jackson, would never have been identified from the prints he left at the site of the crime had his identified prints not already been on Scotland Yard's fingerprint register. Such registers, however, could not be compiled without a system of classifying fingerprint patterns – imagine producing a dictionary without alphabetization. For long, this seemed to be an insoluble problem. Herschel had tried unavailingly to classify fingerprints and Faulds, for all his pioneering vision and for all his claims to have adapted fingerprinting for police work, had not placed any complete system of fingerprint identification in the public domain. Even the brilliant scientific mind of Francis Galton could not discover a simple enough way to organize fingerprints

– which, of course, was the only reason why the Troup Committee did not recommend the exclusive use of fingerprints for criminal identification.

Within a few years of the Troup report, however, everything changed. Identification procedures were transformed root and branch by the introduction of a reliable, efficient and user-friendly system for classifying fingerprints. Once this was available, there was no longer any need to retain anthropometric measurements – which required far more work to record accurately than fingerprints – for the purpose of classifying criminal records.

As with Herschel's initial experiments, it is, once again, the story of an Englishman faced with the daunting task of managing the Empire: Edward Henry (1850–1931), who began his career as a junior clerk at Lloyd's in London and ended it in 1918 as Sir Edward Henry, Commissioner of the Metropolitan Police.

Bored to tears by the life of a clerk, he took evening classes at University College London, where he developed an interest in law. In 1871, he entered the Society of the Middle Temple for formal legal training. Passing the competitive examination for entering the Indian Civil Service in 1873, he was posted as collector and assistant magistrate in Herschel's Bengal and had, by 1890, risen to the secretaryship of the Board of Revenue. None of these initial posts satisfied his legal interests – although they did give him ample time to play polo, participate in amateur dramatics and hunt jackals (Bengal, alas, had no foxes) – and he was to come into his own only when appointed Inspector General of the Bengal Police in 1891.

In the decade that he spent in this post, Henry made history. First, he made anthropometry a routine part of Indian police practice. Anthropometric measurements, of course, had been in use in India for some time – it was the favoured method of anthropologists to determine racial and caste types and was

FIGURE 19
Sir Edward Henry.

introduced during the Ethnographic Survey of Bengal in 1886. Since Indian caste groups did not intermarry, the study of their measurable physical features, it was argued, would identify each caste in 'scientific', numerical terms. Herbert Risley, a pioneer of the anthropometry of caste, declared that if a series of castes were arranged in the order of the average nasal index (the relation of the breadth of the nose to its height), 'so that the caste with the finest nose shall be at the top and that with the coarsest nose at the bottom of the list, it will be found that this order substantially corresponds with the accepted order of social precedence'. The bodily dimensions revealed the social order.

Edgar Thurston, author of the classic, seven-volume *Castes and Tribes of Southern India* (1909) and curator of the Museum in Madras, was so keen on the anthropometric study of racial characteristics that he frequently pounced on museum visitors – not, of course, on the white visitors but only on the 'natives' – with his calipers. Introducing him at a lecture at the Royal Society of the Arts in London, Lord Ampthill reminisced: 'A visit to the Government Museum at Madras was always a very pleasant experience, although at first alarming. Such was the author's zeal for anthropometry, that he seized every man, woman, or child in order to measure them'. Thurston himself complained later that his measuring instruments frightened the natives, 'especially the goniometer for determining facial angle, which is mistaken for an instrument of torture'. A small fee to the measuree, therefore, was eminently advisable as also 'cheroots for men, cigarettes for children, and, as a last resource, alcohol'. Thurston's faith in the eloquence of physical features such as the nasal index was as deep as Risley's: intelligence, he averred, varied 'in inverse proportion to the breadth of the nose'. Many others throughout India pursued the great task of anthropometric measurement with equal, if less startlingly manifested devotion.

The goal of the project was to identify and label the major *types* of the population, not individuals. Nor, of course, were these anthropometric measurements classified in a Bertillon scheme. Nevertheless, colonial theories of caste and race proved crucial to the introduction of anthropometric identification in police work in India. Colonial anthropologists revelled in delineating – some might say inventing – tribes or races with distinct physical and spiritual characteristics. The Rajputs and Sikhs of western India, for instance, were supposedly distinguished by matchless physical courage and their valiant, warlike nature. These, in the parlance of colonial ethnography, were 'the martial races' of India. But racial concepts were not enough to explain the characteristics of Indians. As every British administrator knew, India was the land of caste, where every priest, every warrior, every scribe pursued his trade not because he had *chosen* it as a vocation but because he was *born* into a family that had pursued the same trade for all time. The Indian Muslim's choice of profession – caste was and is unique to Hinduism, the faith of the Indian majority but not of every Indian – was left out of these theories, which silently assumed Indian to mean Hindu.

The Indian criminal was equally explainable in the light of caste. In this strange land, crime, too, was a hereditary pursuit: criminals did not act in the way they did from choice but because they were born to it. (In Lombroso's theory of the born criminal, it was a question purely of biological inheritance – in colonial explanations of crime in India, inheritance was primarily a cultural matter, albeit hardened into something almost biological in its inflexibility and predictability.) Groups of criminals in India were organized, according to colonial policemen and administrators, into specific tribes functioning as castes. Most curiously, criminal tribes were sometimes acknowledged to be of indigenous royal lineage – which did not surprise colonial administrators because the native royals, of course, were little better than criminals.

The eminent jurist James Fitzjames Stephen defined the criminal tribe or caste (the terms remained interchangeable) in 1870 in words that rang through the years, striking dread into the hearts of administrators. 'Trades', Stephen explained,

> go by castes in India; a family of carpenters now will be a family of carpenters a century or five centuries hence ... If we only keep this in mind when we speak of 'professional criminals', we shall then realise what the term really does mean. It means a tribe whose ancestors were criminals from time immemorial, who are themselves destined by the usages of caste to commit crime and whose descendants will be offenders against the law, until the whole tribe is exterminated or accounted for ... Therefore when a man tells you that he is a *Buddhuk* or a *Kunjar* or a *Sunoria* he tells you what few Europeans ever thoroughly realise – that he is an offender against the law and has been so from the beginning and will be so to the end, that reform is impossible for it is his trade, his caste, I may say his religion to commit crime.

Stephen's words were novel and striking but the concept itself was not. At least from the 1860s, British administrators had evolved ways to exercise surveillance over the nomadic, idle and violent criminal tribes. In one district of the Punjab, for example, the Commissioner recommended that each member of three designated tribes should be registered at local police stations, that the headmen of the villages where these people lived be ordered to pay security deposits to the police and obliged to report the movements of the villagers to the police. The registered persons would be permitted to leave their villages only if they had a ticket-of-leave from the police. As a gesture toward the reclamation of these tribes into civil society, it was also recommended that local landholders be encouraged to provide the tribesmen with land. Turning them into peasants was the obvious way to wean them away from their inborn criminality – an idea charming in its inconsistency with ideas of the inflexibility of caste.

The courts, however, rejected such measures of surveillance and reclamation, insisting that the Indian Penal Code already offered sufficient means to deal with all kinds of criminals. The 'native police', moreover, were considered infinitely corruptible by the courts: surveillance by them could never succeed. The lure of sharing in the criminals' ill-gotten wealth would give them the courage to disregard all government instructions. Administrators grumbled and fumed at this judicial interference. 'If a shepherd saw a wolf coming out of its den, he would not wait until there was tangible proof that his flock was in danger', one of them thundered. What did judges know of the depredations committed by these tribes? Courts, in any case, should confine themselves to judging committed crimes rather than interfere with crime prevention. Nevertheless, the legal difficulties were insuperable and the surveillance techniques had to be withdrawn.

But concerns over criminal tribes did not cease. After years of debates, localized attempts and reams of memoranda, the Criminal Tribes Act finally went on the statute book in 1871, ordering 'the registration, surveillance and control' of these tribes. Their reputation for moving around the country, thieving and pillaging wherever they went, made them 'the gypsies of India' and the new law decreed that they should be confined to distinct settlements and a complete register of the tribes was to be maintained by the district magistrate. Members of the tribe were confined to their village or town, and if they wanted to travel they had to apply to the police for a pass, which recorded their residence, the places they were allowed to visit, how long they were permitted to be absent from their domicile, and the police stations where they would have to report periodically while travelling. Even those who did not wish to travel were subject to periodic roll-calls by the magistrate and a *daily* inspection by the village headman, each evening. Magistrates were given the power to order tribal residences to be searched on suspicion and to order the arrest – without warrant – of any tribal member straying beyond the ambit of his pass. Even a village headman could make this arrest and headmen and landholders were obliged – under the threat of punishment – to inform 'the nearest police station of the arrival of any person who may reasonably be suspected of belonging to any tribe, class or gang'. A member of such a tribe or group violating the boundaries determined by his pass was liable to six months of rigorous imprisonment – a British-Indian term for penal servitude that is still standard in India – or to a fine and whipping, even if he had not committed any criminal offence. With a second violation of the limits of movement, the punishment was a year's rigorous imprisonment *and* a fine *and* the whip.

Colonial administrators took a very dim view of nomadism of any kind: people with no fixed residence came automatically under suspicion of being criminals and one of the primary aims of the Criminal Tribes Act was to force roving and supposedly dishonest bands into settled, productive cultivators. Hence, the Act allowed the government to resettle designated criminal tribes where they could be compelled to adopt productive practices such as agriculture. The resettlement plans of the government, however, never worked particularly well and it remained, on the whole, more a pious objective than a realized or even a realizable goal. Resettling tribes and converting them into agriculturists required arable land – and the expense proved a strong disincentive for enforcing the Act. Later, in the early twentieth century, institutional options were also tried: reformatories were established for the purpose, some of them run by the Salvation Army.

Reform, not surprisingly, proved more difficult than surveillance. Edward Henry pointed out in 1891 that successful reclamation of criminal tribes 'has proved in practice ... insurmountable', not least because of the expense involved in resettling nomadic tribes on cultivable land. But pessimistic as he was about reclamation, Henry was enthusiastic in applying Bertillonage to identify members of criminal tribes straying from their settlements. (Ethnologists such as Thurston were often called in to train policemen to take these measurements.) In his early assignments as magistrate to different parts of the huge Bengal presidency, Edward Henry had often encountered the problem of confining the criminal tribes to one location and precise anthropometric identification of each individual seemed to him to be the best way to achieve the government's object. 'With anthropometry on a sound basis professional criminals of this type', he claimed, 'will cease to flourish, as under the rules all persons not identified must be measured, and reference concerning them made to the Central Bureau'.

Apart from the issue of the criminal tribes, the government had no intention of ignoring individual habitual criminals – inconsistent as always, colonialists, in suitable circumstances, could forget their conviction of every profession in India being based on caste – defined as 'any person convicted on two or more occasions of offences' of specific kinds defined by the Indian Penal Code. In a reprise of debates over criminal tribes and the need for surveillance, government officials again engaged in a prolonged correspondence on the subject in the 1880s. Again, mobility was what administrators were anxious to control and the railway, otherwise the most resplendent jewel in the crown of the British Raj and held up regularly as a great justification for British dominion over India, was blamed for making a bad situation worse. The Secretary to the Government of the Punjab explained, 'the development of the railways and the increased means of procuring employment at a distance from their homes, has rendered the loose characters more able and willing to leave their villages . . . The offender is not bound thereby to remain in any particular locality, and neither by inclination nor by the difficulty of communications is he precluded from seeking new

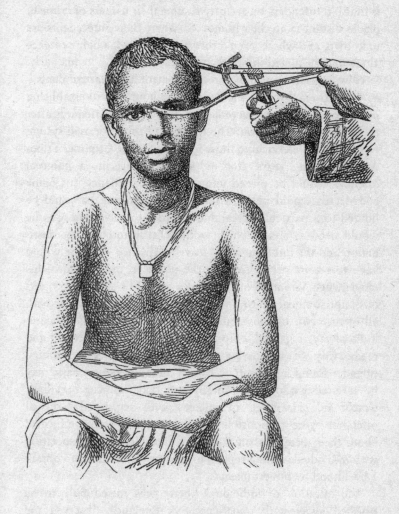

FIGURE 20
Bertillonage in Bengal.

scenes wherein to indulge in his criminal propensities. The result is that old offenders on security resume their careers of crime in places distant from their homes . . . where their antecedents are unknown, and where, even if they are convicted, a light sentence alone may be meted out to them'.

New legislation was required to control habitual criminals – as with criminal tribes, the need of the hour was to establish a meticulous 'system of surveillance', especially of offenders after their release from prison. The features of this proposed system were virtually identical to those instituted in the Criminal Tribes Act: for some years after release from prison, a habitual offender would be placed under police surveillance, his name and details would be on a register, his movements would be limited to a particular area, and in order to leave that area he would need a pass – which would clearly indicate his destination and the duration of his leave of absence – and he would have to report periodically to the police in the course of his movements. Violators of these rules would be subject to rigorous imprisonment up to a year, or a fine, or whipping, 'or with all or any two of those punishments'. (The colonial police in India always regarded whip marks on the back as a rough and ready way of identifying repeat offenders.) Any habitual offender found 'anywhere in British India' without a pass 'may be arrested without warrant by any Police officer or village watchman'. Headmen of villages with registered habitual offenders were responsible for keeping the police informed about their 'being absent at night without leave, or association with individuals of bad repute, or ceasing to labour or to obtain a livelihood by honest means'.

The question of individual liberty was raised only to be brushed away with impatience. 'In England', observed the Inspector General of the Punjab Police, 'an habitual offender, on conviction, is invariably sentenced to a term of Police surveillance . . . If this procedure has been found necessary in

England, where the liberty of the subject is most jealously guarded, I can see no reason why it should not be introduced in this country'. If, moreover, the government had deemed it necessary to limit the liberty of 'persons who by the misfortunes of their birth are members of a criminal tribe, but who have themselves never been convicted of an offence, how much more important is it to impose some check on the liberty of persons who have shown themselves to be habitual criminals and to be enemies of society at large'. A magistrate wrote from northern India: 'In every country of Europe, I believe, even in countries like France and Italy living under democratic institutions, sur-veillance of a far more rigorous character [than in England] is permitted by the law. And it must be remembered that in European countries the Government in its struggle against crime ... has the whole of the non-criminal population on its side, whereas in India very few have any idea of public duty, and most men shrink from incurring danger or trouble by assisting the police ... The respectable classes of this country are timid, and the *badmashes* [crooks] often establish a reign of terror'.

Then, in 1890, relatively late in the course of the correspon-dence, the all-important question raised its head. 'It seems to me', suggested A. E. Staley, a Bengal magistrate, 'that too little stress has hitherto been laid on the necessity of finding means to identify habitual criminals'. So far, he reminded the govern-ment, the procedures for the identification of habitual offenders had been 'of the feeblest'. His list should have made instructive reading: '(a) parade before the *local* police at *local* jails on Sundays, (b) accidental recognition by jail and police officers, (c) descriptive rolls in *Police Gazettes*. The first two are almost entirely ineffectual. The descriptive rolls in *Police Gazettes* are insufficient. It involves a great expense of time to look them up. A man's attention must necessarily flag when reading through a great number of separate unclassified items of description'. In short, the system in India, although not different in essence from the one then in force in England, was even more rudimentary and disorganized. What was the use of introducing legislation on surveillance when one did not possess a reliable means of identifying the people to be put under surveillance? 'There are 236 habituals now on our rolls in this district who are supposed to be under surveillance, but who are at large in some place unknown, and probably engaged in crime'. One method of identification that might have helped was some kind of tattooing – this had indeed been common in the early days of Company rule, when those sentenced to life imprisonment were tattooed on their foreheads with name and offence, but it had been discontinued by the mid-nineteenth century and was considered too brutal to be reintroduced.

Even if a flawless method could be found to identify individuals, it would not, in itself, suffice for the identification of habitual offenders unless its data could be organized in a searchable database. This, of course, was the crux of the matter and even in England, the police had not, as yet, found such a system. Something of an enthusiast for photography, Staley had earlier urged the government to consider adopting 'the ferrotype process of photography for multiplying identical photos of the faces of habitual criminals' and now advocated that the photographs be used to supplement a classification based on 'measurements of parts which do not vary; the size of the skull over the head from the junction of ear to ear, the length of the ulna [one of the bones of the forearm]'. Also in 1890, a judge from northern India told the government that identification was the crucial issue and that 'the French system of anthropometry is believed to be singularly effective' in identifying repeat offenders. Staley, however, was even more advanced: an index arranged by measurements should, he advocated, be subclassified by 'the impression of the thumb, and personal marks'. Such ideas would have been considered advanced (perhaps too advanced) even in England at this time.

In India, however, they should have been old hat by now. Herschel's contributions, if properly developed and adapted for police purposes, would have made Indian identification procedures far superior to European methods long before the 1890s. As we have seen, however, not only did Herschel's innovation fail to spread in India, it even died out in his own district after his departure. Consequently, criminal identification in India remained primitive and had to start afresh with Bertillon. If history had progressed on the straight, rationalistic line so beloved of old-style historians of science, then India – and Britain itself – should not even have needed to pass through the anthropometric stage. But that was not how it happened.

Soon after being appointed the Inspector General of the Bengal Police in 1891, Edward Henry submitted a plan for the introduction of anthropometry into the Bengal Police for the systematic identification of all habitual criminals – including 'convicted members of ... criminal tribes'. The anthropometric project depended, of course, on the creation of a databank of measurements, which could be used in the future for successful identifications of suspected habitual criminals. Henry's proposal was approved and money was released for the purchase of instruments and other expenses. He immediately trained officers to measure according to the Bertillon scheme and could report in 1892 that 'some 3,000 of the principal criminals in the several jails of the Province have been measured and classification of their cards is now being carried out'. The measuring instruments had been imported from France but even at this early stage, Henry mooted the need to improve them 'to reduce to a minimum the source of error which necessarily arises from the varying personal equation of different measurers'. The next year, these improved instruments were available: 'the calipers and sliding-bar have, by the addition of mechanical appliances, been rendered automatic, the personal equation of the measurer being thereby almost eliminated', Henry reported. 'Over 6,000 cards containing the measurements and all details as to the previous criminality of the most dangerous criminals in the Province have now been classified . . . Generally I may claim that the system has been placed on a sound basis'. The Lieutenant Governor commended Henry for his 'marked zeal and ability', observing that although 'it has not been possible to put the system to any practical test . . . it promises to be of the greatest value in the future'.

The anthropometric system Henry introduced in Bengal was a modified one. Bertillon's system, as we have seen, was not designed for use on non-whites – certain identifying characteristics such as the colour of the eye were obviously unusable in India. As far as the measurements were concerned, too, Henry was economical. Only men were measured (women were excluded under all circumstances, no doubt to avoid creating the impression that the foreign rulers were out to dishonour Indian women) and only six of Bertillon's eleven measures were employed. (In a letter to Galton, Major Ferris of the Indian Army dismissed it as 'a bastard imitation of Bertillonage'.) Even then, a complete measurement could take up to one hour.

When the anthropometric system began to be used for practical identification in 1893, Henry had already added the impression of the left thumb to the anthropometric cards. He had read Galton's 1892 book and was an immediate convert as far as the value of using fingerprints for proving identity was concerned. Many successful identifications were made with the combined card, which, Henry observed, 'warrants the belief that it is being worked on sound lines . . . the use of thumb impressions as the final test in the office of search has been adopted with most gratifying results'. Henry would later gloat that the very system recommended in Britain by the Troup Committee had actually been 'independently introduced more than two years earlier in this province'. Strictly speaking, this was not quite correct: the British system recorded the prints of all ten digits, not just of the left thumb. In all other respects, however, the Bengal procedure was indeed remarkably similar to the one that would be instituted in England in 1894. In both, measurements were used only to locate a card in the register: once a likely record was located, the fingerprints recorded on it were compared to the suspect's. Only if these were identical would identification be considered positive.

'This test has never yet failed us', Henry declared, emphasizing that the possibility that two individuals might have the same fingerprints had been 'demonstrated by experts to be infinitesimally small'. The government happily noted: 'The number of successful identifications thus secured in the eight months up to 1st April 1894 was 48, and it is interesting to compare these figures with the corresponding figures in France, where in the second year of the working of the Bertillon system, the number of successes under similar conditions was only 49'. By the end of the next year, the number had risen in Bengal to 140 – this represented only 23 per cent of all suspected of concealing their identity but it was still an undoubted advance. Anthropometry was introduced in the curriculum of the police training school, where all probationary sub-inspectors (between 120 and 150 were appointed every year) were trained. 'The means now at the disposal of the Bengal Police for dealing with recidivists', Henry declared with tight-lipped pride, 'are more complete than are possessed by the police either in England or in any English colony'. In practice, however, the situation was rather more complicated. The question of discrepancies between measurements taken of the same individual at different times by different operators refused to go away. The standard of measurements in distant jails, where no adequate supervision could be provided on a regular basis, caused perpetual anxiety. In order to allow for inaccuracies in measurement, searches in multiple pigeonholes were essential, which meant that the average time required for a search could often exceed one hour.

PLATE VIII.

I. G.'s Office Serial No. ————	Full name with *aliases*—Abdul Guffur, *alias* Abdul Karim, *alias* Kalloo, *alias* Lalit.
Caste—Shekh.	Religion—Muhammadan.
Mother-tongue—Bengali.	Profession—Tailor.
Father's { Name—Khoda Buksh.	Police-station—Moochipara.
{ Village—Amherst St.	District—Calcutta.

Convictions:—Calcutta, 4 months, 1-10-84, § 380, I. P. C.; (2nd) Dacca, 6 months, 3-10-88, § 457, I. P. C.; (3rd) Hooghly, 1 year, 14-10-91, §§ 379 and 75, I. P. C.

For photograph. Full face.	For photograph. Profile.

		Cent.	Mille.		Cent.	Mille.
Head. { Length		19	1	Left forearm	46	7
{ Width		14	6	„ foot	24	8
					Feet.	Inches.
Left middle finger 11			1	Height	5	6

Peculiarities of speech, gait, appearance, etc.—Medium complexion. The last phalange of the left little finger is deformed owing to a cut received in boyhood. Humpbacked.

Age on 12-10-92 between 35 and 40 years.

FIGURE 21

Bengal's answer to the Bertillon fiche.

Marks and Scars.

Head, face and neck—A large wart on centre of right cheek, 4 cm. from nostril and 6 cm. perpendicularly below the outer corner of right eye.

Arms—Large scar on right forearm, anterior, 4 × 3 cm. in size, 18 cm. above tip of middle finger.

Breast and belly—Black patch or birth mark on breast, 18 cm. above navel, 4 cm. to the right.

Back—Scar, 3 × 2 cm. in size, 7 cm. from the 7th vertebra and 3 cm. to the left.

Thighs and legs—Cut, 4 cm. long, on right thigh, anterior, 34 cm. above ground.

Measured on the 12-10-92, at Alipore Jail, by Md. Khurshed.

Tested on the 12-10-92, at Alipore Jail, by Mr. W. A. Gayer, Assistant District Superintendent of Police.

Entered in Jail Register on the 12-10-92. Admission Register.

No. 1349.

> MOHAMMAD KHURSHED, Special Sub-Inspector,
> *Signature of measuring officer.*

From now on, Henry would be in regular communication with Galton. Visiting Galton's laboratory on a trip home in 1894, he showed him his anthropometric instruments. 'He measured my head breadth ten times', Galton recorded, 'I showed him much about finger prints . . .' At this point and for at least a while longer, Henry does not seem to have harboured any serious misgivings about anthropometry in itself; he was anxious only about eliminating the discrepancies between measurements. 'I am satisfied with our results from anthropometry', he wrote to Galton in 1896, 'but the supervision needed to ensure success is a strain and as possibly my successor may take less interest in the subject I am anxious to substitute a system which affords less scope for errors. We measure now at about 120 centres, so exercising supervision is no light task'. That same year, however, he reported to the government that notwithstanding the success of anthropometry,

> the substitution of finger impressions for measurements, if a satisfactory system of classifying them can be devised, would yield even better results than we are now getting. The cost of working such a system would be less, as measuring instruments are not needed; no skill on the part of the operators would be required; the error due to the personal equation of the operator would be a negligible quantity, and finally there could be no errors of transcription of results.

He had already issued instructions that from now on, the single finger impression on the anthropometric card would not suffice – a separate card bearing prints of all ten fingers would also have to be sent to the Central Office, where efforts were under way to evolve a reliable classification of fingerprints.

In 1897, Henry issued a triumphant proclamation. He had at last found the holy grail of identification: a workable system of fingerprint classification. Considering the gravity of the discovery, his announcement was remarkably low-key: 'The considerable advantages which identification by finger impressions would possess over Anthropometry . . . a commencement was made more than two years ago, in working out a scheme of classification by which duplicates of the impressions of the ten digits could be rapidly and unerringly traced. The many difficulties met with have been overcome . . .' The announcement had been preceded by an examination of Henry's system by two experts (the Surveyor-General of India, Major General Charles Strahan, and the scientist-educator Alexander Pedler, FRS) appointed by the Government of India. They had reiterated the weaknesses of the anthropometric system, noting the simplicity of recording fingerprints and the proof of identity they provided: 'The greatest sceptic would be at once convinced of identity on being shown the original and duplicate impressions. The exact repetition of most minute details is quite astonishing. There is no possible margin of error, and there are no doubtful cases'. All this, of course, was nothing new: the Troup Committee had been equally eloquent in endorsing the identifying attributes of finger marks.

What had stunned the Indian government's experts and what was unprecedented in the British experience, however, was the new system of classification. Marvelling at the speed with which it allowed anybody to find the duplicate of a specimen print in the large collection, they exclaimed: 'We were both able to find the originals of two of the most intricate cards that could be produced, with ease and certainty. The men whose duty it is to look up the originals, in no case took more than five minutes to produce the original'. Consequently, they had unhesitatingly recommended the discontinuation of the anthropometric system and the adoption of fingerprinting as the sole method of identification. On 12 June 1897, the Governor-General in Council commanded that 'the system of identification of criminals by finger impressions is to be adopted generally in British India' and by the end of the century, it had spread far beyond Bengal, being in use in Bombay, Madras, Punjab, the North-Western and Central Provinces and even in Burma, where anthropometry itself had never been used. Together, these regions had a population of about two hundred million people, and over the years their police forces had collected about two hundred thousand anthropometric cards, which were now to be replaced with fingerprint data as far and as quickly as possible.

What, then, was the system of classification that had brought about this massive change in policy? It began with a rigidly standardized method of recording the prints. First, the fingers were rolled from side to side on the ink and then pressed similarly on the paper. There was nothing new about rolling itself: Galton himself had recommended it because it ensured that the complete ridge pattern, including that on the edges of the fingers, would be on record. The rolled impressions were taken in strict order: right thumb, right index, middle, ring and little fingers, and then the digits on the left hand in identical order. Plain prints (in which the fingers were not rolled, the print recording only the central portions of the pattern) of the same fingers in the same order were then taken on the lower part of the paper. This was a precautionary measure: since the rolled prints were taken separately, it was conceivable that the operator could mistakenly record a right index finger impression, for example, as that from the right middle finger. The plain prints, therefore, were taken after placing the index, middle and ring fingers in 'a tin guard or mitten with strap, which keeps them in a fixed position, leaving exposed their first phalanges': this ensured that the prints were taken together and could not be confused. (This was an innovation and was unknown in Britain then as well as later.) The rolled prints were used for the classification but always compared with the plain prints to ensure accuracy.

After the prints had been taken, their patterns were recorded in pairs, beginning with the right thumb and right index fingers and ending with the left ring and left little finger. Henry had adopted Galton's basic division of ridge patterns into arches, loops and whorls, but added a fourth type called composites. As the name suggests, a composite was a print which combined features of more than one of the three Galtonian patterns. It had been found that approximately 5 per cent of all patterns were arches, 60 per cent were loops and 35 per cent were whorls and composites. Henry's primary classification, therefore, subsumed the smaller category of arches into the far bigger one of loops and the composites were included with the whorls. Using this scheme, one could, as shown in the appendix, spell out *all* possible combinations of patterns for a pair of digits. And there were only 1,024 possible combinations. Since 1,024 was the square of thirty-two, 'a cabinet containing thirty-two sets of thirty-two pigeon-holes arranged horizontally would provide locations for all combinations of Loops and Whorls of the ten digits taken in pairs'.

One oft-repeated story claims that the idea of a classification system for ten-digit prints had come to Henry in a flash while staring out of the window of an express train to Calcutta – not having any paper on him, he immediately jotted down his idea on his starched cuff. Another version, attributed to Henry himself by Sir Basil Thomson in his *History of Scotland Yard*, claims that the epiphanic moment came while he was 'riding through the Indian jungle'. The real genesis of the system, however, may have been more complicated. It is well known that Henry had two Indian assistants, both sub-inspectors, Azizul Haque and Hem Chandra Bose, and while they did not leave any known account of their time with Henry, there is some evidence to suggest that their contributions to the development of the 'Henry system' amounted to more than mere assistance.

Haque, in particular, is supposed to have played an important role in helping Henry evolve the system of 1,024 pigeon-

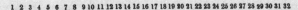

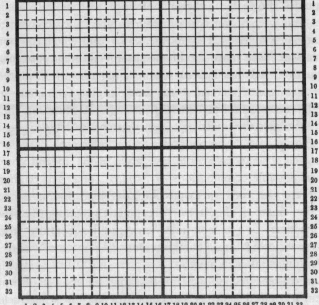

EXPLANATION.

The impressions of the ten digits are taken in pairs in the following order:—

(1) Right Thumb and Right Index; (2) Right Middle and Right Ring; (3) Right Little and Left Thumb; (4) Left Index and Left Middle; (5) Left Ring and Left Little.

Key.

All impressions are held to be divisible into 2 types, Loops (which include Arches) and Whorls. Given ten impressions in the above order, they can be expressed by some such formula as the following:— LW-WL-LL-WW-LW where $L =$ Loop; $W =$ Whorl. The Key indicates the one pigeon-hole out of the 1024 of the Bureau where a card with the above formula will be found. Referring to the Key, LW is in top right hand square, therefore we proceed to square defined by the broad continuous lines, and by the horizontal numbers 17 to 32 and vertical 1 to 16. Taking the next pair WL we see from the Key that it is in bottom left square of $\frac{17-32}{1-16}$, i. e.; in the square defined by continuous and broken broad lines and by horizontal figures 17—24 and vertical 9—16. The next pair LL is in left top corner of this $\frac{17-24}{9-16}$ square, i. e., in the square defined by one broad continuous, one broad broken, and two medium continuous lines, and by horizontal figures 17—20 and vertical 9—12. The next pair WW is in right hand bottom corner of this $\frac{17-20}{9-12}$ square, i.e., in square marked by two broken and two continuous lines and by horizontal figures 19—20 and vertical 11—12. Finally, the last pair LW is in top right hand corner of this $\frac{19-20}{11-12}$ square, i.e., is in pigeon-hole $\frac{20}{11}$. Any other combination of impressions can be similarly located.

FIGURE 22

The Bengal pigeonhole system for classifying fingerprints.

holes and the mathematical formula that determined which pigeonhole a specific card was located in. (A murkier story has it that Haque, in turn, was assisted in constructing the formula by an anonymous professor of mathematics at Calcutta's leading college.) The most damning anecdote of all is that when Haque drafted a classification scheme and gave it to Henry, the Inspector General 'studied it for a week but failed to understand it'. (The source, an article published in the 1950s in the *Patna Journal of Medicine*, cites no sources for this claim and goes on to assert that once Henry had mastered the classification, he 'sent the report to England, admitting the help he had received from Haque. The report was approved'. There was no such report and this inaccuracy does not strengthen one's faith in the more sensational claim made in the article.) Much of the story, unfortunately, depends on hearsay and has been circulated without any documentation by fingerprint experts such as John Berry and Stephen Haylock. The meagre documentary evidence – unearthed by the historian Radhika Singha – relates to Haque's application for a land grant at the time of his retirement in the mid-1920s. His claim to be one of the originators of the fingerprint classification system was investigated at the time and Henry himself declared that Haque had 'contributed more than any member of my staff and contributed in a conspicuous degree to bringing about the perfecting of a system of classification that has stood the test of time and has been accepted by most countries'. Sir Douglas Gordon, a former Inspector General of the Bengal Police, wrote to *The Times* in 1965 that Henry had 'placed on special duty two Indian Inspectors' to work out 'a formula or set of formulae which would enable prints to be classified ... This in due course they succeeded in doing and the result of their labours and ingenuity is the basis of the "Henry" system which he brought with him to London when he was appointed Assistant Commissioner at Scotland Yard'. Gordon had known both Haque and Bose during his days in the Bengal Police and although by 1965 he could no longer recall their names, he strongly implied that they and not Henry created the classification. The full credit for the system, he declared, 'rests with the Bengal Police'. This was supported by a subsequent letter to *The Times* from H. C. Mitchell, the Honorary Secretary of the Indian Police (UK) Association. Mitchell asserted that it had been Haque who, in 1897, had explained the classification to the government committee investigating the utility of fingerprinting. 'Retired officers of the Indian Police', he stressed, 'are anxious that the work of Azizul Haque and Hem Chandra Bose should be commemorated and that their names should be on record in India and in this country'.

Mitchell also reported that Henry, when dining with Bengal Police officers during a visit to India in 1912 (Henry accompanied King George V and Queen Mary to the Coronation Durbar in Delhi as special equerry and security adviser), spoke in glowing terms of Haque and Bose. (As usual, there is a variant of the story, in which the climax comes with the 'presentation by Sir Edward to the assembled company of his former Sub Inspector of Police Khan Bahadur Azizul Haque – the man mainly responsible for the new world-wide fingerprint system of identification'.) Haque received the title of Khan Sahib from the government in 1913 and that of Khan Bahadur in 1924. These titles were decorations for Indian Muslims – and not, as so many Western writers on the subject seem to assume, parts of Haque's name – and since not many Indian subinspectors ever received such high honours, it is likely that Henry had recommended him for these decorations. Similarly Bose received the decoration Rai Sahib and later Rai Bahadur – the Hindu counterparts of the honours received by Haque. Both also received honoraria of 5,000 rupees each for their contributions to the establishment of fingerprint identification.

There is no incontrovertible evidence that either Haque or

Bose ever felt slighted by Henry. Indeed, on the title page of Bose's 1916 book, *Hints on Finger-Prints with a Telegraphic Code for Finger Impressions*, he described himself as 'Finger-Print Expert, Pupil of Sir Edward Henry, Commissioner of Police, London, and Founder of the Finger-Print System of Identification in India'. It is certainly possible that being still in the imperial police service, Bose and Haque may have been hampered by professional fears from expressing their grievances toward a British superior, even after he had left India. There is, sadly, nothing intrinsically implausible or even unlikely about a colonial official taking the credit for the contributions of his Indian assistants. The 'He Nicked It' scenario may well be true but before we completely rewrite the history of the Henry classification, we need more authoritative evidence than we currently possess. All that *this* evidence allows us to say is that Henry was probably not as appreciative of his two Indian assistants as they may have deserved. (And of course, one should probably take the story of the express-train epiphany with more than a grain of salt.)

The system, whatever its origins, ran exceedingly well in practice. Prints of convicts were taken in jails and forwarded to the Central Office in Calcutta with all other particulars of the individuals that were known or stated. At the Central Office, the prints were classified by one officer, verified by another, and then filed in the respective pigeonholes. When prints of suspects were sent to the Central Office asking for identification, the same procedure was followed for the classification of the submitted print, and then the cabinet was searched for a match. Since it was conceivable that the finer subclassification of the original prints might be slightly different from the one decided on by the classifier of the suspect's prints, cards in the adjacent subgroups were also examined. Multiple searching, however, was far quicker with prints than with measurements. Even an exhaustive search of 30,000 cards could be completed within five to six minutes. 'A practised person', Henry declared, 'carries photographed on his eye the salient features of the slip [i.e. fingerprint card] he is looking for, and can search for it as rapidly as his hand is able to turn over the Record slips'. Finally, in 1911, that quintessentially colonial law, the Criminal Tribes Act, was amended to include fingerprinting of all members of designated criminal tribes over the age of twelve.

The Bengal classification of fingerprints was a landmark not merely in colonial history but in the international history of identification. Although Juan Vucetich of Argentina (also inspired by Galton's research), had developed his own scheme for classifying the impressions of ten fingers by 1891, it was only in 1904 that the Argentine police adopted fingerprinting as the sole method of identification. Many South American nations soon followed the Argentine lead and for long, many experts considered Vucetich's classification to be actually superior to Henry's. Nevertheless, Vucetich's system never had any impact anywhere in the English-speaking world, perhaps largely because his works were never translated into English. The Henry classification, on the other hand, took British India by storm in the 1890s and a little later, Britain itself and the United States.

The triumph of fingerprinting in British India during the 1890s, however, was not confined to the identification of criminals. Virtually simultaneously, the civil arena witnessed the second coming, so to speak, of Sir William James Herschel. The impetus for this came, ultimately, from the work of Francis Galton. Once Galton's requests for samples and evidence reawakened Herschel's memories of old exploits and unfulfilled dreams, the baronet made one final effort to revive the use of fingerprints in civil identification. Bengal, at the end of the nineteenth century, was no longer run by people who would treat his suggestions with disdain and later apologize at parties. His friends and appreciative subordinates were now at the helm of affairs, in particular Henry Cotton, the Chief Secretary to the Government of Bengal. He had regained his urge to speak and there were powerful people now who might listen.

In 1892, Herschel, at Galton's request, asked Cotton to organize the collection of prints from his old Hooghly register and from a few of the original individuals who might still be found. He also sent Cotton a copy of Galton's book on finger-prints. Cotton not only obtained the prints requested but also sent Herschel one of Henry's reports, pointing out that in the anthropometric identification system now in regular police use in Bengal, the print of the left thumb was used to establish identity. Simultaneously, the current magistrate of Hooghly, entrusted with collecting fresh prints from Herschel's old sub-jects, reported to Cotton that 'I think and have long thought that it would be an excellent thing to insist on the taking of prints in the Registration Department. Every year I have been in the country, I have come across cases of denial of execution involving a great expenditure of time, money and false swear-ing. There can be no doubt that personation for the purpose of registering documents is rather a common offence, and that this system would absolutely cut it out'.

Cotton quoted this remark to Herbert Holmwood, the Inspector-General of Registration, observing, 'You are probably aware of what Herschel did in this direction when he was at Hooghly some fifteen years ago, and he now suggests that his methods should be again tried for purposes of identification in the Registration Department. I do not know whether you will look on the scheme as a practical one or not . . . I commend the whole subject to your attention and believe it will repay you your trouble'. Cotton's copy of Galton's book was enclosed with this letter. Although he had done his best for his beloved old boss, Cotton, however, was not terribly optimistic about the possibilities, warning Herschel not to be 'too sanguine': 'I have never been one of those who think we can show the way to the Heads of Departments in Europe. If they try the experiment and it succeeds then we can follow in India'.

Cotton would have to eat his words soon. Holmwood turned out to be very receptive to the idea of using fingerprints for identification – and for essentially the same reasons that Herschel had developed it. 'The question of false personation', Holmwood declared, 'is a most important one; and all native gentlemen . . . agree that it is still of everyday occurrence and no system has hitherto been devised capable of checking it. I have . . . seen the wonderful results collected by Sir W. Herschel at Hooghly and verified in eight cases only the other day . . . and I am convinced that the system would in a very short time put a stop to all attempts at false personation in registration offices. The absolute certainty of detection, as soon as the courts realise the scientific basis of the system, would inevitably prevent any attempt to personate another person'. In May 1893, the Political Department of the Government of Bengal issued orders for the introduction of 'Sir William Herschel's system for securing the identification of parties and their witnesses in the registration of deeds', initially for Calcutta and adjoining areas, including Hooghly, where, of course, it had all begun. In 1896, fingerprint signatures were also officially adopted in the Pensions Department.

'It is a very great pleasure to see my one accidental discovery turn out useful,' a moved Herschel wrote to Cotton. 'Thanks to Galton and yourself for rescuing it'. Modestly giving all credit to Henry and Holmwood, Cotton nonetheless assured Herschel that 'as long as I am in office out here it will receive every encouragement from government'. And so it did. Within a year, Cotton wrote to Herschel announcing, 'your labours in the matter of finger prints have borne fruit in Bengal . . . both in the Registration and Police Departments, your system is now being followed with great success'.

Soon, of course, the Bengal Police also abandoned anthro-

𝕲𝖔𝖇𝖊𝖗𝖓𝖒𝖊𝖓𝖙
of 𝕭𝖊𝖓𝖌𝖆𝖑. } **1893.** { **POLITICAL**
DEPT.

REGISTRATION.

MAY.   File $\frac{I}{I}$

Nos. 1-2.

Introduction of Sir William Herschel's system for securing
the identification of parties and their witnesses in the
registration of deeds.

LIST OF PAPERS.

1. Letter from the Inspector-General of Registration, No. 1737, dated
   the 7th April 1893, proposing to introduce tentatively in the
   districts of Calcutta, the 24-Parganas and Hooghly, Sir William
   Herschel's scheme for securing the identification of parties and
   their witnesses in the registration of deeds, and submitting for
   approval a rule which it is suggested should be added to Rule
   48 of the Registration Rules.

2. Letter to the Inspector-General of Registration, No. 1468P., dated
   the 2nd May 1893, sanctioning the addition of a Rule to Rule
   48 of the rules framed under section 69 of Act III of 1877.

FIGURE 23

The second coming of Sir William James Herschel – the Government
of Bengal wakes up to the merits of fingerprinting in the 1890s.

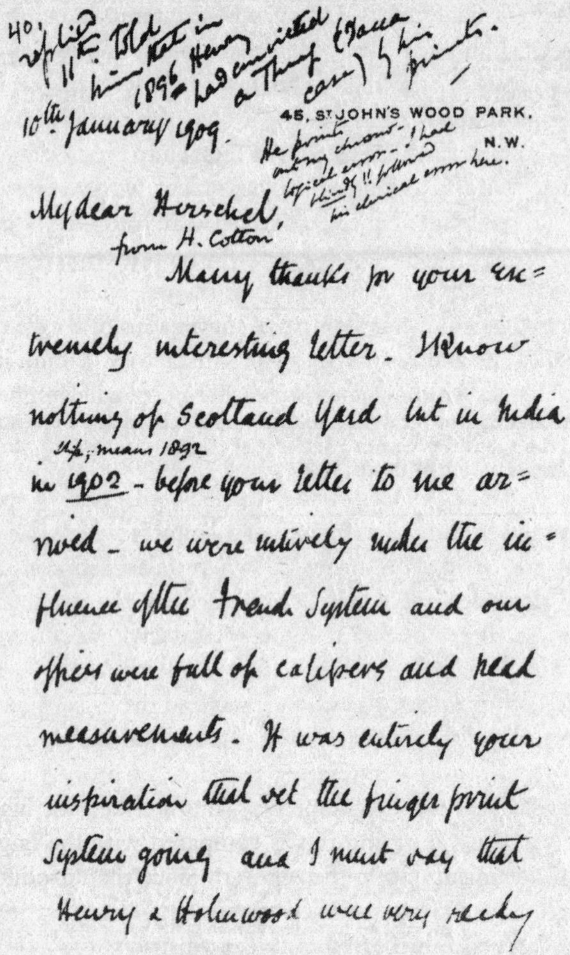

40. replied 11th. Told him that in 1896 Henry had convicted a Thief (Bana case) by his prints.

10th January 1909.

45, St. John's Wood Park.
N.W.

He points out my chronological error — I had thought it followed his clerical error here.

My dear Herschel,
from H. Cotton

Many thanks for your extremely interesting letter. I know nothing of Scotland Yard but in India in 1902 (Mis; means 1892) – before your letter to me arrived – we were entirely under the influence of the French system and our offices were full of calipers and head measurements. It was entirely your inspiration that set the finger print system going and I must say that Henry & Holmwood were very ready

FIGURE 24

Henry Cotton's 1909 letter to Herschel, declaring: 'before your letter to me arrived – we were entirely under the influence of the French system and our offices were full of calipers and head measurements. It was entirely your inspiration that set the finger print system going . . .'

pometry for fingerprints. Henry, whose interest in fingerprinting had been stimulated not by Herschel himself but by Galton, also paid homage to the man who was now well on his way to immortalization as the founding father of fingerprinting. Referring to Herschel's 1892 request to Cotton to see whether fingerprinting could be adopted in government work, Henry wrote, 'you will see by the papers I forward that your wishes have not been lost sight of and that your important discovery is likely to have even wider applications than you anticipated . . . I am at present engaged in classifying the impressions of the 10 digits of 5000 persons and results are most satisfactory. I think it highly probable that Anthropometric measurements will be superseded, even in the Police Department, by Finger impressions, and then your system will have achieved a very remarkable triumph'.

Fingerprinting, Henry later emphasized, was 'particularly well suited to the requirements of a country where the mass of the people are uneducated, and where false personation is an evil which even the penalties provided by the penal laws are powerless to control'. All military and civil pensioners were now fingerprinted; this simple step had worked wonders, he reported, in preventing pension fraud and the use of fingerprinting in the registration of deeds had put a stop to the venerable Indian tradition of repudiating transfers of property. In cases of repudiation, the executant was simply asked for his fingerprint 'in open Court and this is compared with the impression on the document and in the register'. Since the introduction of the technique, Henry claimed in his annual report for 1897, 'cases have been instituted in twenty districts for false personation and convictions obtained in twenty-five cases, in which sentences varying from seven years to six months have been inflicted'.

Even more uncannily reminiscent of Herschel's experience during the Indigo Revolts was the use of fingerprinting in the Opium Department. Since the eighteenth-century beginnings of

British rule in India, and until 1914, the government held a monopoly on the cultivation and sale (primarily to China) of opium. This open involvement of a British government in the drug trade had always been criticized (especially in England) but it brought in too much revenue to be dispensed with. As with indigo, opium was cultivated by *ryots* who were not particularly fond of the crop and were often forced into growing it by the agents of the government. Advances, as Edward Henry summarized in 1900, were 'made on account to the cultivators through middlemen, the poppy crop being hypothecated as security. If the middleman or the cultivator proves dishonest, the issue is raised whether particular sums reached the persons they were intended for'. Cultivators frequently disowned genuine contracts, and equally frequently, contracts were forged by middlemen. This had finally come to an end because 'the finger impression of the payee is now required to authenticate acknowledgment of receipt'.

Equally redolent of Empire was the use of fingerprints to authenticate contracts signed under the Emigration Act. Since the end of slavery, India had been one of the sources for the supply of indentured labour to the rest of the British Empire. This system depended on the worker signing a bond agreeing to serve in a foreign country for a number of years. Recruiters frequently resorted to ruses to entice illiterate villagers into signing such bonds – fraudulent contracts were common and so were repudiations of contract by labourers who discovered too late the falsity of the stories of untold riches and wonderful lives in foreign climes. The use of fingerprints on the bond resolved the situation and the indenture system, a typically colonial product and a close cousin of slavery, was saved from collapse.

Many ordinary employers, too, now authenticated the payment of advances or salaries to employees by asking them for their fingerprints on the receipt. Huge organizations such as the

Survey of India maintained registers of their employees' thumb impressions and 'if a particular man is dismissed for misbehaviour, a photo-zincograph of his impression is sent to all the working parties, which ensures that he cannot again get taken on, even by assuming a false name'. Recently, even the Post Office had begun to register the thumb impressions of its many thousands of employees, and officers of the Medical Department of the Bengal Presidency stopped issuing medical certificates without recording the thumb impression of the patient. In public examinations for government employment, impersonation was common – 'the candidate who appears in the Examination Hall not being the person who secured the certificate entitling him to compete' – and candidates for the examination to appoint Sub-Inspectors in the Bengal Police had been asked to provide their thumb impressions. Henry hoped that this would soon become a requirement in all competitive examinations for public jobs.

The needs of imperial administration, however, were far from exhausted by these uses: 'In connection with the administration of the rules for preventing the spread of plague, and for regulating the pilgrimage of Mussulmans [Muslims] to Mecca, certificates are authenticated by bearing the thumb impression of the persons to whom they are granted'. But even more could be done. Since death did not immediately obliterate the ridge patterns, Henry regretted that insurance offices had not yet begun to use them to determine the identity of the dead, although he acknowledged that this reluctance might be due to the fact that in India, 'bodies are buried or burnt almost as soon as death occurs'. Others found ever more creative ways to use the novel technique. In Bombay, those applying for jobs as municipal sweepers had to submit to fingerprinting and these prints were examined by the Fingerprint Bureau to identify those with a criminal past. But fingerprinting was of use even with people under no suspicion – from 1895, the postal services in India used the fingerprints of illiterate people on money order receipts and postal savings accounts. Even today, an Indian money order receipt asks for the 'left thumb impression' from recipients who cannot sign their name.

Indigo, opium, indentured labour, pension scams, registration fraud, impersonation in examinations, plague prevention – the needs of Empire were unique as well as numerous. The potential applications of fingerprinting in colonial administration, as Herschel had realized years earlier, were boundless. Perhaps the greatest value of finger impressions in a caste-ridden, religiously divided land like India was that, as Henry put it, 'no objection can be raised on the ground of religion or caste, or rank in society, or sex, so there is no prejudice to be overcome in obtaining it'. This glorious vindication of every single claim he had ever made for the utility of fingerprinting must have made Sir William Herschel's heart sing.

In the criminal domain, however, things were somewhat more uncertain in the early years. The intrinsic value of the technique was not in dispute. What was not so clear was who had the final say in pronouncing a positive match between fingerprints. Fingerprint identification – especially from imperfect prints left at a scene of crime – was hardly a task for the untrained, nor was the new classification navigable without some familiarity with its principles. One had to be something of an expert to testify convincingly on a fingerprint match (or lack of it) in the courts. The law of evidence in British India, however, had been promulgated in the Indian Evidence Act 1872, and Section 45 clearly specified the categories of expert witness whose evidence was admissible in criminal cases. These were 'persons specially skilled in . . . foreign law, science or art, or in questions as to identity of handwriting'. In the otherwise obscure 1896 case of *Queen Empress* v. *Fakir Mahomed Sheikh, Arshad Ali Shaha and Sitanath Das*, it was realized that this definition of expert witness excluded the police expert on fingerprint identification. Fakir Mahomed, a wealthy man of a Bengal village, had presented a document for registration, the fingerprints on which, according to the complainant Noyan Shah, were forged. (As we know, fingerprints were now de rigueur in the registration of deeds.) The Sessions Judge of Nadia – that district where Herschel, in the midst of the Indigo Revolts, had found his hobby to hold the key to administrative salvation – allowed a police expert to tell the court that the prints on the deed did not match those of the person they were supposed to be of. The jury was divided: three were for acquittal, two for a conviction. The judge favoured the minority view and referred the case to the High Court, where it was considered by one European and one Indian judge.

Justice O'Kinealy decided that the fingerprint matching should have been done by the judge himself and therefore, was in favour of acquitting the accused. Justice Banerjee agreed, adding interesting observations on the nature of fingerprint evidence. Citing Galton, he accepted that 'those who have made finger prints their special study have come to the conclusion that their similarity is, as a rule, evidence of personal identity and their dissimilarity will, therefore as a rule, be evidence of the reverse'. A comparison of fingerprints to determine identity would, therefore, be legally permissible but 'such comparison must be made by the Court itself; and the opinion of an expert as to the similarity of such impression is not admissible under Sec. 45 of the Evidence Act'. Nothing was wrong with the technique itself but the law did not recognize the fingerprint expert.

This verdict caused a flutter in legal as well as government circles. The Government of India proposed to amend the Evidence Act to admit expert evidence on fingerprints. The legal profession clearly wanted to retain its authority on the comparison of prints. 'Mr Henry may undoubtedly be regarded as an expert in the matter, but we are not aware of the existence of any other experts in India', remarked the *Calcutta Weekly Notes* (no obscure journal but the voice of the Calcutta High Court, an institution hailed by a British MP as 'the noblest manifestation of British justice') in 1898. 'But will it be practicable to call Mr Henry as witness all over the country? If not, will it be safe to allow the prosecution to produce supposed experts from all ranks of police officers in this country to prove identity by this means?'

An 'inspector, a sub-inspector, a head constable or a rural registrar or sub-registrar' was, the *Weekly Notes* agreed, capable of recording fingerprints correctly. It refused, however, to accept that such foot-soldiers of law enforcement could ever acquire genuine expertise in *interpreting* fingerprints. Moreover, it emphasized, 'we know how police testimony even with regard to ordinary identification is unsatisfactory and not infrequently open to abuse. The subordinate police officers in this country do not enjoy a good reputation'.

British judges in India had an inveterate distrust for lower-ranking Indian policemen. As Edmund Cox recorded in his 1911 treatise *Police and Crime in India*, 'the police in India are of the people. With whatever care they are selected, whatever training they may be given, it is impossible to suppose they can be free from their national traits, inclinations, and weaknesses. Any judge or magistrate will admit that in Indian courts of justice the class of people whose evidence is looked upon with the greatest suspicion is the police'. This suspicion stemmed, ultimately, from the general conviction of the intrinsic mendacity of Indians. Sessions judges in India, for instance, had been given the authority to demand the police diary, which recorded all facts and statements pertaining to an inquiry. No English judge had this power and there was no suggestion that he should. India, however, was a different world, where the ordinary policeman was dishonest enough to alter or concoct evidence and ignore evidence challenging the prosecution case.

It was hardly surprising, therefore, that the legal establishment was so unwilling to give such policemen the right to provide expert evidence to courts on as crucial an issue as identification. Fortunately, as the Fakir Mahomed case revealed, there was a solution. Expert evidence on fingerprints should be treated merely as corroborative evidence 'from which the judge or the jury draw legitimate conclusions in each case'. Final authority on deciding the identity of prints, in short, belonged to the Court, not to the police expert.

The new legislation resolved the issue amicably. As Henry himself put it, the government had been so convinced of the value of fingerprinting that with Act V of 1899 amending the Indian Evidence Act of 1872, 'the testimony of those who by study have become proficient in finger-print decipherment' had been accepted as expert evidence. At the same time, the new law had amended another section of the old Act, permitting Courts, as the *Calcutta Weekly Notes* was delighted to point out, 'to compare finger prints and to take finger impressions from persons present in Court for the purpose of comparison'. Gloating in its victory, it went on to expatiate that 'there is no special charm in the expression "expert evidence" as the novelty of it in this country might lead us to think ... Judges in England and America have often declared experts to be the least satisfactory of witnesses and it is no wonder that they have many a time come to the conclusion that it is always safer for the Court to rely on their own judgment'. Everyone had won and all had received prizes.

The use of fingerprints in the identification of criminals and the detection of crime now took off rapidly. In 1893, the first year of the practical application of anthropometry, 23 identifications had been proved in court; in 1896, the last year when measurements were used, there were 334 successful identifications. From June 1897, new convicts were no longer measured – only their finger impressions were kept on record. At the end of that year, 174 successful identifications could be attributed to the fingerprint-only system; next year, the system had 345 successes. Several of these identifications, Henry pointed out, could never have been made on the basis of the anthropometric measurements on record because the original record and current measurements varied so greatly as to 'frustrate all chance of successful search'. The Central Office, at the end of the century, held records for 48,000 criminals, 32,000 of which were fingerprint records only, and it was envisaged that the older anthropometric records would be gradually eliminated altogether. Henry went on trips around India to train different police forces on the collection and classification of prints, leading to its early adoption in regions beyond Bengal. Herschel would later salute Henry's achievement by dedicating his booklet *Origin of Finger-Printing* to him and declaring his 'warm and continuous admiration of those masterly developments' that had transformed his original, administrative tool into 'a weapon of penetrating certainty for the sterner needs of Justice'.

Soon, fingerprint evidence figured prominently in a lurid case of murder. In August 1897, Hriday Nath Ghosh, the manager of a tea garden in the northernmost district of Bengal, was found murdered in his bedroom. A safe in the room had been forced and a substantial amount of money taken from it. At first, there were many suspects. The manager was known to be an oppressive boss and the labourers on the tea estate, it was thought, could well have killed him in sheer desperation. Or the relatives of his mistress might have done it to avenge family dishonour. A local gang of moneylenders suspected of criminal activities was also suspected. A former cook of Ghosh's, who had been caught six months earlier stealing money from that very safe and sentenced to six months in jail, was also reported to have declared that he would wreak vengeance on Ghosh after his release. This man had been released in July 1897 – to mark the Diamond Jubilee of Queen Victoria – and had subse-

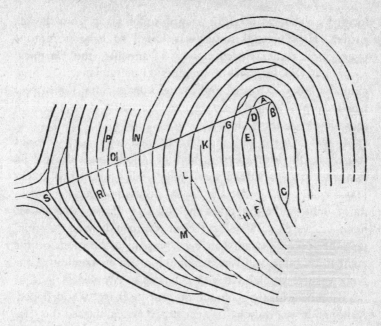

FIGURE 25

Evidence of identity in the first murder case turning on
fingerprint identification, northern Bengal, 1897.

quently been seen by many around the tea garden. His right
thumb impression had been recorded before he was released
from jail.

The police found an almanac inside a box in the victim's
room, which had a couple of brown smudges on its cover – this
was sent to the Central Office in Calcutta. One of the smudges
turned out to be the mark of a right thumb. The files were
searched and an impression was found that matched the one on
the almanac – the fingerprint on file was that of the former
cook.

The man had by now disappeared but the police finally

located him at his home, a long distance away from the tea garden. His financial status was found to have undergone unexpected recent improvement. Meanwhile, the Chemical Examiner reported that the smudges on the almanac had been made by blood. Arrested and brought to Calcutta, the suspect was fingerprinted and once again, there was a perfect fit with those found on the almanac.

He was charged with murder and theft at the local sessions court, pleading not guilty to both. The judge was assisted by two assessors – all three were Indian. They refused to accept that a charge of murder against the accused could be substantiated only by the marks on the almanac. Those same marks, however, were considered sufficient to prove 'beyond question' that the former servant had been present in the room on the night in question and 'the presumption that he committed the theft was irresistible'. He was sentenced to two years' rigorous imprisonment for the theft and the murder charge was dropped. Although it was only half a success, Henry publicized this case prominently in his book as illustrating the potential of the fingerprint system and, perhaps, implying very subtly that only the ignorance of the judge and the assessors had prevented a murder conviction. The odds against all the similarities found between the prints on the almanac, the print on file and the print taken actually from the man himself occurring in impressions from two different individuals, Henry calculated, were more than a million to one.

Other successes were reported from regions beyond Bengal. In Mathura in northern India, one Man Singh was accused in 1901 of murdering a wealthy acquaintance called Durga Pershad. A brass pot was found near the body with a bloody finger mark 'with the whorls and ridges plainly marked'. Although Man Singh had been arrested on other evidence, the print on the brass pot was found to be identical to his own by a police expert. Criminals, the expert explained, 'are identified by fingerprints only now. The measurement system is only in use for the old cases, in which no finger prints have been taken. I have been employed in this work for three years. All cases from North-Western Provinces, Punjab, Bengal, Madras, and Bombay come to me ... I never saw the impression of one man's fingers the same as those of another. They may be alike, but there is always some difference'. This expert witness – an Indian – was treated with great respect by the judges, who remarked that through his hands 'every year thousands of finger impressions pass'; his evidence was evidence 'upon which we can safely rely'. The defence called witnesses testifying that the accused was elsewhere on the day of the murder. The judges were so impressed by the fingerprint evidence, however, that this evidence was dismissed summarily. 'In this land of lies an ounce of good circumstance is worth many pounds of oral evidence', declared one of the judges; even if two hundred witnesses had sworn to the alibi, 'it would be as nothing in my mind compared with the unexplained bloody thumb print'. The fingerprint expert, clearly, had quickly acquired considerable authority in the eye of judges.

But not universal, unquestioned authority. Not as yet. Legal objections could relate, for instance, to the manner of recording the evidence or interpreting it – and we shall see that ordinary jurymen could be far more sceptical about interpretation than judges or magistrates. The 1904 case of *Emperor* v. *Sahdeo*, a criminal appeal (against the guilty verdict of the district magistrate) before H. J. Stanyon, the Additional Judicial Commissioner of the Central Provinces, turned on the recording of evidence and the identity of persons whose prints were purportedly recorded on the fingerprint slips used by the police. Well versed in the complexities of individual identification and familiar with Galton's *Finger Prints*, Stanyon asserted that fingerprints were 'an absolutely certain mode of identification, wherever the materials for its application are present ... The exact differences in such impressions can be pointed out with as much certainty as the differences between the maps of two countries'. But was there similar absolute certainty that the marks in the police database had indeed been made by the person named on the records? This was not a trivial issue. Sahdeo, the accused, had been arrested after a recent theft, to which he pleaded guilty. On the basis of fingerprint evidence, however, the police identified him as responsible for five previous offences, all of which he denied, and all of which were attributed to a person called Kamta. Although he had no doubts about the matching of the patterns or about the qualifications of the expert witness, Stanyon considered it unsound and uncertain to assume that the recorded fingerprints, with which the accused's prints were matched, had indeed been made by the individual who had committed the five previous crimes.

Expert evidence could attest to the identity of *prints* but not to the identity of the *persons* making the prints. 'The finger prints of B on the back of a slip drawn up for A may be impressed without difficulty if there is no safe-guarding of the process', argued Stanyon. 'I should not be at all surprised to hear that incidences of this kind have already occurred ... If signatures need attestation or certificate, surely the necessity is equally great in the case of finger prints. What is there in the present case to rebut the suggestion that the accused, as a joke, or as an act of friendship towards Kamta, put his finger prints on the paper?' He, therefore, returned the case to the district magistrate, asking him to retrieve the records of the previous cases and confirm, from records of paternity, age and so forth and from interviews with policemen familiar with Kamta, that Sahdeo was indeed Kamta. 'I am aware', he emphasized, 'that the taking of this evidence will make the finger print evidence practically superfluous: but this is unavoidable, though much to be regretted. A good and useful purpose will have been served if in future the record of finger prints is made ... in a duly authorized public document, containing certificates from which it may be legally presumed, *prima facie* – (a) that the prints are those of the person whose they are, in the document, stated to be; and (b) that when he made them, such person had been previously convicted (if at all) as stated in the impression record'. As it happened, further investigations established that Sahdeo was indeed Kamta and his appeal was dismissed, but the point made by Stanyon was more than a legal quibble.

The other kind of legal objection – that related to the interpretation of fingerprint evidence – was at the heart of the 1905 case of *Emperor* v. *Abdul Hamid*, a criminal appeal tried at the Calcutta High Court. Abdul Hamid had allegedly impersonated Moshrof Ali and executed a bond defrauding the latter. As usual, the registration records carried fingerprints and Sub-Inspector Mahomed Amin of the Central Office in Calcutta testified that the prints on the bond and the prints in the register maintained by the Registration Office were identical to those of the accused but not to those of Moshrof Ali, who had ostensibly executed the bond. The jury, however, unanimously decided that Abdul Hamid was not guilty, at which the perplexed judge asked them whether they considered the prints of the bond not to match the prints of Abdul Hamid. 'We are not ready', the jury declared, 'to accept the evidence of the expert as conclusive. We do not think he is properly qualified to give an opinion'. The patently disgusted judge referred the case to the High Court with the statement that the jury's opinion was 'absolutely and utterly unreasonable'. Distrust of the expert police witness, therefore, was not the monopoly of judges. Juries could be even more recalcitrant.

Mr Justice Henderson, one of the judges deciding on the appeal, acknowledged that the expert witness had extensive training as well as experience in fingerprint identification and was 'entitled to be treated with very great consideration'. But he was not willing to take his word for it. 'I have myself subjected the impressions to a careful study both with the naked eye and a magnifying glass', he announced. (This, of course, was permitted by the amendment of the Indian Evidence Act.) Upon examining the prints, Henderson found that they were 'unfortunately blurred and many of the characteristic marks are, therefore, far from clear . . . I am unable to say more than that in some respects a distinct similarity can be traced'. The expert's opinion was certainly worthy of respect but if the judge or jury could not verify it, then, Henderson implied, the expert testimony should be disregarded. 'I should hesitate', he concluded, 'before I would convict on the mere result of a critical examination of thumb impressions made by an expert. I know nothing about the particular expert witness . . . The Jury had an opportunity (the Judge, of course, had also) of seeing the witness and judging of his manner of giving evidence, and it may be that they were honestly of opinion that they could not trust his evidence'. The original verdict, Henderson thought, should be allowed to stand and the accused acquitted.

The other appeal judge, Justice Geidt, also refused to overturn the original verdict but added considerably to Henderson's observations on evidence, expertise and interpretation. The classification of fingerprint patterns, he allowed, was 'a science requiring study' and special expertise might be required to pronounce any two fingerprints as identical. Once that identification had been made, however, the points on which it had been made could be 'weighed by any intelligent person with good powers of eyesight'. Like his colleague, he, too, had examined the prints in the case and although the pattern and the central core were identical in both sets, the expert had defined seven other points of identity which he had been unable to verify. 'For instance', he pointed out, 'the Sub-Inspector's second reason [for arguing a match] is that the number of ridges between the right delta and the inner terminus is the same. The Sub-Inspector has not mentioned the number of ridges thus indicated, and they are so blurred and run together, that I am unable to count them for myself'. Some of the expert's other points he could discern in one print but not in the other.

Geidt then moved to themes beyond the technical. 'The Sub-Inspector', he observed, 'is a person who failed for his B.A. Examination, and has been only a little more than a year in the Police. Considering the difficulty I have in perceiving the marks which lead him to [claim identity of the two sets of impressions], I cannot say that the Jury were wrong in declining to regard him as an expert, whose opinion they were bound to accept without the corroboration of their own intelligence as to the reasons which guided him to his conclusion'. Carefully pointing out that he did not harbour any doubt about the validity of fingerprint identification, he emphasized nonetheless that he did not consider that the expert evidence was of sufficient weight to 'disturb the verdict of the Jury'. Learned justices were under no compulsion to bow to the authority of a mere policeman even on a subject that seemed, at least at first glance, to be as rebarbatively technical as the identification of fingerprints.

There was another potential problem with the extensive use of fingerprinting, although it does not seem to have raised too many ripples: the possibility of forging prints. In Britain, *The Red Thumb Mark* (1907), Richard Austin Freeman's first novel featuring the medico-legal expert Dr John Evelyn Thorndyke, turned on this very question, and in the denouement, Thorndyke stuns judge and jury by producing a mould constructed in his workshop that duplicated a fingerprint flawlessly. Rebuking the police for regarding the fingerprint as a 'magical touchstone, a final proof, beyond which inquiry need not go', he declares that fingerprint evidence 'in the absence of corroboration, is absolutely worthless. Of all forms of forgery, the forgery of a finger-print is the easiest and most secure, as you have seen in this court today'. The discovery of a print at a scene of crime, therefore, did not necessarily prove that it had been left by the person whose ridge patterns it matched. Earlier, Sherlock

Holmes, in *The Adventure of the Norwood Builder* (1903), had demonstrated to Inspector Lestrade – predictably a fervent believer in fingerprint evidence – that what was supposedly the guilty man's thumb mark on a wall had actually been planted by the real culprit. Although there was some speculation amongst fingerprint experts on the possibility of forgery and frequent allusions to *The Red Thumb Mark*, most authorities seem to have pronounced definitively against it fairly early on – the doubts of fictional detectives and their creators caused some debate but never impeded the triumphal progress of fingerprinting in Britain. And even the detectives came to heel pretty swiftly. By 1911, Holmes, on finding a scrap of paper with a bit torn off in *The Adventure of the Red Circle*, observes like a true believer that 'there was evidently some mark, some thumb-print, something which might give a clue to the person's identity'. And that arch-sceptic Dr Thorndyke, in now unjustly forgotten later novels (such as *The Mystery of Angelina Frood* or *Pontifex, Son and Thorndyke*) happily relies on fingerprints to identify individuals without worrying at all that the prints might be forged. In the 1932 story *When Rogues Fall Out*, we even learn to our surprise that a portable fingerprint apparatus is part of the 'permanent equipment' of the green-baize-covered research case emblematic of the Doctor.

In India itself, however, fears of fingerprint forgery were more intense. The medical jurist Lieutenant Colonel Henry Smith reported in a 1930 lecture at the Medico-Legal Society in London that during his years of service in India he had come across forged fingerprints and had himself experimented with various methods. He claimed that he was able to transfer a fingerprint from one piece of paper to another either by lithography or simply by compressing the original print against a damp sheet and then compressing the latter onto another damp sheet. 'I supplied', he recounted, 'originals, negatives and positives of these to the Government . . . At once the result was that telegraphic instructions were issued to everyone who had any-thing to do with finger-prints that these must be witnessed in future, just as a man's "mark" is witnessed'.

Smith's lecture and, especially, the discussion following it tell us much about the way the development and use of fingerprint-ing were tied inextricably to ideas about the duplicitous nature of Indians. The eminent judge Lord Atkin, a former president of the Medico-Legal Society, observed after Smith's talk that in dealing with appeals from India, he had noticed that 'India appears to be ... the home of forgery of all kinds'. Another member of the audience, the medical jurist and writer C. Ainsworth Mitchell, agreed that 'the forgery of the finger-prints used as a safeguard upon documents in India had become almost a fine art, the natives having invented a method of transferring them by means of the intestinal skin of the young goat'. And yet, as Lord Atkin put it, in a country where '97 per cent' of the population was illiterate, 'the very greatest import-ance must be attached to finger-prints, for the purpose of authenticating documents'. But Indians were not to be con-trolled that easily. 'There is no doubt, I think there can be no doubt at all, but that in India they do not stick at forgery on the small scale', he sadly noted, sharing details of some of the recent Indian appeals he had judged, all of which had involved forged signatures and documents. One adoption document, he recalled, had been signed by nine witnesses supposedly present at the ceremony but the document 'was found by the Court below to have been a complete invention. There had been no ceremony of adoption and there had been no deed, and these persons were not present there at all, and their signatures were forgeries'.

In 1936, the Calcutta-based fingerprint expert Frank Brew-ester declared that Herschel's original effort to get an artist to reproduce fingerprints had failed simply because 'in those days the processes employed for transferring designs to paper were far short of the mechanical perfection of to-day'. Things were very different now: 'It is doubtful if there is any other country in the world in which fingerprints are so extensively used as signatures for everyday business transactions as in India. Consequently, the opportunities of the forger are almost unlimited, of which some wily persons are not slow to take advantage'. Brewester contended that it was easy for 'one who knows' to reproduce fingerprints so perfectly as to deceive an expert, even though he would not, of course, reveal those techniques. (He dismissed Henry Smith's damp paper method as good in theory but useless in practice: mere damp paper, Brewester argued, could not 'lift' enough of the inked original to reproduce it.) Afghan moneylenders supposedly from Kabul, he reported, had evolved a powerful technique to forge prints: 'Instead of using damped paper, the Kabulis employ special substances to obtain the negative impression. The cost of the requisite substances is trifling, the method of operating is simple, and the results very satisfactory – from the point of view of the forger. The results are so good that they are dangerous, and it is believed that . . . Kabulis victimised many persons who had the misfortune to get into their clutches'. (The so-called Kabulis were held to be responsible for a whole constellation of petty crime in colonial India, not just dishonest moneylending.) He recounted the case of a Bengali, who, expecting to be fined by a court, had borrowed thirty rupees from a Kabuli, agreeing to pay the moneylender the usual interest. In order to save some money in stamp fees, the Bengali signed two bonds, each for fifteen rupees, and affixed his thumb impression to both. On finding that he was not, after all, to be fined, he returned to the Kabuli with the money and the interest that had accrued, took the bonds back and destroyed them. After some months, he received a lawyer's letter stating that he had borrowed six hundred rupees from the Kabuli and had repaid only fifty – the moneylender refused to wait for any longer for repayment and would institute a civil suit against him if the loan was not immediately cleared. The Bengali, knowing he hadn't borrowed that money, ignored the letter.

Soon, however, he was staggered to be summoned to court, where the Kabuli produced a bond, swearing it had been signed by the Bengali, whose thumb impression it bore. 'The usual "cloud of witnesses" ably supported [the Kabuli], all of them telling their stories in such a way that they fitted together like a jig-saw puzzle. Not a ray of light came through the crannies and crevices of their stories', narrated Brewester. One odd thing about the bond, however, was that it contained two thumb marks, 'one much lighter in shade than the other'. The Bengali denied they were made by him but when officers from the Fingerprint Bureau were called, they pronounced the prints to be identical to his own. The court reached the likely verdict and the Bengali was ruined financially after repaying the alleged debt. And *then*, he received another lawyer's letter stating that his loan of seven hundred rupees was now overdue and he would be taken to court if he did not pay up. Again, the bond had two impressions of a thumb and the Bengali now declared that the bond must be a forgery.

'By means of that extra sense which many Indians seem to possess', Brewester continued, the Bengali discovered another moneylender who was a sworn enemy of his supposed creditor. Unwilling to forgo the opportunity to injure his rival, the second moneylender revealed to the Bengali how the forgeries were committed, providing so much information that the indebted man was soon an adept at the art and demonstrated it at court, when summoned on the second charge. The stunned judge dismissed the suit but the Kabuli forger had, by then, absconded. After the trial, Kabuli moneylenders, according to Brewester, became far more careful and the practice died out.

In spite of the tussle between the judges and the police and questions surrounding forgery, the validity of the fundamental *principle* of fingerprint identification – that the patterns on the fingertips are unique to the individual and persist through life and hence ideally suited for the identification of individuals – does not seem to have been challenged in India. In actual practice in the civil realm, however, fingerprints do not seem to have been regularly investigated by matching and in spite of the popularity of the technique, no national register of fingerprints was ever compiled in India. The thumb mark was little more than a signature the supposed unfalsifiability of which was rarely tested in practice. Nevertheless, it was used so extensively that by the end of the nineteenth century – less than fifty years after Herschel's original brainwave – India had become finger-print-land. Britain itself, however, lagged far behind its colony. In 1894, an incredulous Henry Cotton had asked Herschel, 'I wonder if in these matters we are in advance of the Police in England: is it possible?' The answer could only be an unequivocal yes. The bigger question, of course, was whether the mother country would employ this colonial invention to resolve its own hardly trivial dilemmas over identification.

SIX

Coming Home

In Britain, the identification of criminals was still a problem at the end of the nineteenth century. The measurements-plus-fingerprints scheme recommended by the Troup Committee had been instituted but for a variety of reasons, many of them related to legal difficulties and administrative complexities, it had not been used as extensively as expected. In 1895, Charles Troup himself had privately confided to Francis Galton that all was not well with the combined system recommended by his committee a year before: 'From what I hear I fear the work is not being pushed on very zealously or vigorously'. In 1900, therefore, the Secretary of State for the Home Department again appointed a committee to look into the issue of criminal identification in Britain and recommend whether the current system needed to be changed. Chaired by Lord Belper (Henry Strutt, second Baron Belper – immortalized in all recent histories of fingerprinting under the ludicrous label of Lord Henry Belper), the Committee comprised, among others, Frederick Bosanquet, the Common Sergeant of London who would later sentence the burglar Harry Jackson, and the chairman of the previous committee, Charles Edward Troup.

The very first witness examined by the Belper Committee was Edward Henry, and he came with the proofs of his book, *Classification and Uses of Finger Prints*. Justifiably claiming extensive experience with anthropometric as well as fingerprint systems of identification – nobody else in the British Empire could match Henry's knowledge of using either system on its own for so long – Henry expressed his disenchantment with anthropometry far more strongly than he ever had on his official reports or even in his private correspondence. The reason the Bertillon system was unsatisfactory was not because of any inherent conceptual flaw but because 'you cannot depend at intervals of time on two different measurers getting exactly the same measurements of the same subject . . . I maintain that it is impossible to take accurate measurements'. And this despite the precision of his redesigned instruments, which, Henry cleverly pointed out, had been admired for their precision by Galton himself. He maintained an eloquent silence when the Committee enquired whether the Bertillon system might serve simply as a means of classifying the cards as they currently did in Britain with fingerprints the deciding point of identification. Contrary to the assertions of some historians, however, Henry did not – whether before the Committee or elsewhere – describe the system as inherently inapplicable to non-Europeans. Nor did he blame the anthropometric system's failures on his Indian measurers.

Henry then proceeded to explain his system of fingerprint classification to the Committee. Admitting that one still needed experience to differentiate between doubtful patterns, he pointed out that even in the most indeterminate cases, the number of pigeonholes that might need to be searched never became anywhere as large as with anthropometric classification. When the Committee suggested that Henry's classification of fingerprints was 'the same as Mr Galton's, with some modifications', Henry firmly replied: 'No, he classifies in another way entirely . . . he classifies by suffixes. I showed my classification to him and he said it was extremely ingenious'. Careful not to seem too brash, however, he quickly added: 'I have followed Mr Galton where I possibly could. It is entirely due to him that the system was started at all. In order to get rid of those gradational cases in which the patterns were doubtful I had to have a fourfold classification instead of a threefold classification'. Of his Indian assistants there was no mention. When asked whether his classification system was his own invention, Henry answered unhesitatingly, 'Yes.'

The Committee was greatly impressed by Henry's carefully trimmed and embellished report of the north Bengal murder and the role fingerprint evidence played in it. He revealed that he had been 'inspecting up the line' and when he had asked the police whether they had any clues, the officer had shown him everything they had found, including the almanac. 'As soon as I saw that I was able to make out that the marks were probably caused by one of the digits of the right hand – my reason for thinking so was the kind of loop'. Having, with these additional details, established how clear fingerprint evidence could be – not to mention how hands-on he was as Inspector General – and judiciously omitting to mention that in spite of fingerprint evidence a conviction for murder had eluded the police, Henry moved on to the most spectacular portion of his evidence.

Trundling a large trunk into the presence of Lord Belper's committee, Henry produced a set of 7,000 fingerprint cards brought from India and demonstrated his classification to the Committee. Following the strategy he had used with the two-member committee of the Government of India, he now invited the members to try their hand at locating prints in the set. 'As far as we could test it with this collection', the Committee reported later, 'it seemed to give excellent results, and to enable a card to be picked out with ease and rapidity . . . we think that it is capable of extension to the point of dealing with 100,000 cases or more without material diminution of the certainty of the results and the ease with which it works'.

Not every witness examined by the Committee, however, had enough faith in fingerprints to advocate their *exclusive* use in identification by the police. The weightiest supporter of the combined system was none other than the seventy-eight-year-old Francis Galton. Recounting his ongoing experiences with fingerprint classification, Galton reminded the Committee that errors of classification were inevitable, 'so you can never say for certain whether the duplicate of a given card does or does not exist in a large collection'. Although agreeing with Lord Belper's view that such errors were inevitable in any method of identification, Galton was in no doubt that 'finger prints alone are less certain than measurements and finger prints combined . . . You have to consider that in 100,000 cases there are 6,000 with ulnar loops on all the fingers – of these 6,000 perhaps half have some notable characteristic, such as a little twist in the middle, but half of them have none, and when you turn over say 3,000 the eye has nothing to fix upon'. The only system that could transcend this difficulty was Galton's own method of counting ridges on three fingers but this, he pointed out, could only be done reliably by experts. 'You want quite a different type of man from an ordinary police sergeant'.

The Committee, well briefed on the imperial situation, pointed out that the Indian police had stopped using measurements because of chronic unreliability. 'Under these circumstances', Galton was asked, 'do you think the importance of having two systems running together is so great that you would continue the system about which there is some uncertainty rather than rely wholly on a system of finger prints if a perfect classification could be discovered?' Galton refused to budge. 'I am timid of making so great a change without more knowledge. France is satisfied with the metric system'. Deeply respected as he was by the Committee, however, the satisfaction of France proved no match for the experience of the British Empire – especially when that experience was transmitted by a representative as successful in his field and as compelling in his presentation as Edward Richard Henry.

Whenever Galton responded lukewarmly to the suggestion that fingerprints might be used exclusively as the basis of criminal identification, the Committee asked him whether he was familiar with Henry's system of classification. 'I regret', Galton replied, 'I have not seen it worked out. One sees that he is fully convinced of its merits, and the Committee in India who reported on it are convinced also, but his book does not go into the subject with sufficient thoroughness to enable me to form a judgment of my own'. The Committee was not so undecided. 'We had evidence from Mr Henry', Lord Belper informed Galton, 'and he brought us a portmanteau full of finger prints, and we had an opportunity of testing it, and it was very successful'. Charles Troup added: 'We especially tested it with the cases of ten ulnar loops and ten whorls, and found it worked very well'. Galton, the very man who had opened Henry's eyes to the value of fingerprints less than a decade before, had now been overtaken by his disciple.

Dr John Garson, the anthropometric expert of the police, was far more emphatic in arguing for the merits of measurements. In his lengthy, occasionally almost bad-tempered evidence to the Belper Committee, he fought two incompatible battles. First, he claimed that the anthropometric system was decidedly superior to fingerprinting on its own and second, that in order to be effective, the former system needed close and constant supervision by a man of science such as himself – an anthropometric office had to be run as a 'scientific laboratory', not as a police department. Since the Committee had already been deeply impressed by Henry's skilful demonstration of the simplicity of fingerprinting and the reliability of his system of classification, Garson's evidence served only to underline that anthropometry required far more time and labour than a system based entirely on fingerprints. The skilled work of interpretation and classification could be done by relatively few experts at the Central Office and even those experts did not have to be scientists. Garson was finally compelled to agree that *if* a satisfactory system of using fingerprints alone could be worked out, the requisite data could be collected by prison officers after minimal training but he denied that Henry had evolved a watertight system for classifying fingerprints. He had seen only one demonstration given by Henry at the Yard and was struck by how much clearer the prints were in Henry's collection. In Britain, he observed, the prints taken on the anthropometric cards were rarely so distinct and he suggested that the ridges were worn down by hard labour in prison. About 7 per cent of all fingerprints taken in Britain were, he argued, defective. As for the ease of using the classification, the one demonstration given by Henry had been less than stunning: 'Sergeant Steadman gave him one or two cases which he failed to find'. When he tried the classification himself, he found that the presence of two defective prints might necessitate searches in forty-three separate pigeonholes.

The many gradations of the patterns, Garson was convinced, ruled out the construction of any classification scheme for fingerprints that could be used as a register of criminal records: 'That is not only my own experience. I have enquired carefully, and it is the universal experience in the office that you cannot always determine and class intermediate forms alike on each occasion, and that means we may have them put in perhaps a great many different systems'. Henry's system did require some ridge counting and ridge tracing for certain categories, work that was far more demanding than taking accurate anthropometric measurements. The primary filing of cards, in short, must be anthropometric with fingerprints being used only for the subclassification of cards. For this latter purpose, he urged the use of 'the fewest number of digits that would suffice' – the first four digits of the right hand rather than all ten digits as used by Henry – and submitted his own system for the consideration of the Committee.

Some of the police witnesses interviewed were also unimpressed by fingerprinting. The City of London Police, it emerged, had no faith even in the anthropometric system. Detective Superintendent McWilliams of that force, instead, argued that his superior, Sir Henry Smith, believed that 'criminals who have been convicted so often that there seems to be no chance of their reformation ought, in the public interest, to be branded'. 'Why should it be necessary', stammered the astounded Committee, 'if you can identify a man with practically absolute certainty by the measurements and finger prints?' 'I don't say we can with absolute certainty', replied the good Superintendent with dignity. The Committee persisted: 'But if the finger prints are absolutely infallible?'

'Sir Henry does not think they are.'

'Has he tried it in one single case?'

'No.'

This, however, was not the norm.

Robert Anderson, Assistant Commissioner of the Metropolitan Police and in charge of identification operations at Scotland Yard, submitted that although he had not yet had sufficient experience with fingerprints to speak with authority and although he would regret the discontinuation of anthropometry, he felt that 'if finger marks could be so classified as to make indexing and searching easy I would give preference to the finger marks'. The Superintendent of the Metropolitan Police's Convict Supervision Office was another strong advocate of Henry's system. Describing it as 'perfect', he exclaimed: 'When it is once in your head you can read it like a book'. Anthropometry was all very well but the system was only as good as the measurers and it was hard to ensure total accuracy in measurements.

Further support for Henry was provided by the Inspector General of the Punjab Police. His conclusions about anthropometry were identical to Henry's and as for fingerprints, he reported: 'We commenced about 1898 recording finger impressions – the two things were run concurrently ... Then men who were working the Bureau found it much easier to proceed by looking at the finger and thumb impressions than to go by the measurement record. In March, 1889, I and other officers attended a meeting held by Mr. Henry, and he showed us his system and produced a record of 7,000 or 8,000, and after a short period of instruction we were able to find the cards wanted; the final result was that the anthropometrical system was superseded by the finger impression system'.

Such strong support from senior policemen of home and Empire made the reservations of Galton, Garson and others seem almost reactionary. The Troup Committee had already declared that fingerprinting would be *the* system for identification of criminals if only a classification could be devised that was simple to use. Now that the Raj had delivered just such a system, the Belper Committee was in a strong position to recommend its exclusive use and the discontinuation of anthropometry. It did not, in fact, recommend such a radical departure in plain language. It did not even dismiss out of hand the value of identification by personal recognition, the examination of photographs, or the sending out of route forms, merely pointing out that they entailed a 'vast amount of labour'. As for anthropometry, the Committee regarded it as a valuable tool, albeit handicapped by the extraordinary precision required by the measurements – 'an error beyond the ordinary margin allowed for variation made in taking or recording a measurement is fatal'. Measurement errors were virtually inevitable, no matter how accurate the instruments and how rigorous the supervision of measurers – consequently, the Committee sighed, 'measurements have been entirely discarded throughout India in favour of a system based on finger prints alone'.

Fingerprints, however, were not only cheap and easy to obtain but, the Committee reiterated, they were 'absolute impressions taken from the body itself, and even though they may be illegible they cannot be incorrect or misleading'. In India, they had proved highly useful not only in the identification of criminals but in such civil contexts as in preventing impersonation of pensioners and the repudiation of contracts. (Oddly, though, the Committee does not seem to have invited submissions on the civil use of fingerprints in India. Herschel, alive and well in Oxford, was mentioned with respect but apparently not even considered as a witness.) Since even in England the combined system recommended by the previous Committee relied on fingerprints to *prove* the identity of a criminal (the measurements being used only for the classification and retrieval of the individual's record), 'the question naturally arises whether they might not be used for classification as well as identification, and if so whether the measurements may not be dispensed with'. Was what was good for the Empire good for England?

Impressive as Henry's classification was, however, the combined system currently in use in England was working well enough not to be discarded

until at all events the Indian system has been given a thorough trial, and is ready to take its place in all respects. Our recommendation, therefore, is that the present system should be maintained for such reasonable time as may be necessary to enable the department to decide how far Mr. Henry's system, with or without any modifications, could safely be adopted, and the present system gradually superseded, but that active steps should be taken towards the immediate introduction of the Henry system. Fingerprints should be taken in all cases on the Henry form and they should be classified according to the Indian system, which should be used concurrently with the other for the purpose of tracing the identity of criminals . . . Unless this experience shows a decisive advantage in the English as compared with the Indian system, the latter will ultimately be adopted, for, other things being equal, the ease with which finger prints can be taken in any place, at any time, and by untrained officers, inclines the balance of advantage decisively in its favour.

The Committee also recommended thoroughgoing reorganization of the administration of the criminal identification system, which was currently handled by the Habitual Criminals Registry at Scotland Yard under the Assistant Commissioner, Robert Anderson, and with Dr Garson as the adviser. One Central Office should instead be set up for the purpose where all the criminal records of the entire United Kingdom would be housed, and the scope of the criminal register should be expanded to include 'all prisoners convicted of indictable crimes and sentenced to imprisonment, whether by Assizes, by Quarter Sessions, or by Courts of Summary Jurisdiction . . . If the police are to be urged to discard their old methods in favour of the new one, no one actively engaged in crime must be allowed to escape the record'. Should fingerprinting be adopted as the only method of identification, the Committee envisaged no legal difficulty. Since the 1871 Prevention of Crimes Act permitted the use of records of previous conviction, there was no obstacle (comparable to the older restrictions in India) to assigning 'the record of the finger prints the same position for the purpose of evidence as is now given to the record of a previous conviction'.

The Home Secretary accepted virtually all of the recommendations of the Committee. The Report itself was never formally published or presented to Parliament as a blue book, however, and today, I know of only one complete copy in the public domain. Almost unannounced to the public or even its representatives, fingerprinting began its short journey to total dominion over identification of criminals in Britain.

The safest way to transplant the imperial technique on home soil was to entrust it to its greatest practical exponent: Edward Henry. From 1899, Henry had begun to attain fame at home – that year, he had addressed the British Association for the

Advancement of Science on his experiences in India in the use of fingerprints in criminal investigation and the next year, he gave his evidence to the Belper Committee. He was then seconded to South Africa, where he organized the civil police of Johannesburg and Pretoria and introduced a new kind of labour pass with fingerprints – to be used, of course, for 'coloured' labourers. (Indians resident in South Africa were required to register their fingerprints from 1902. Later, they, along with Arabs and Chinese, were subject to arrest without warrant if they could not produce their registration certificate with fingerprints on demand. Gandhi himself, then working as an advocate in Johannesburg, protested against these requirements, emphasizing that the use of a technique of criminal registration reduced all 'Asiatics' into criminals.)

Meanwhile, Henry's book *Classification and Uses of Finger Prints* had come out, presenting his system of classification to the entire English-speaking world, 15,000 copies of which had been purchased by the Government of India. In 1901, as the Belper recommendations were accepted by the government, Robert Anderson, the Assistant Commissioner in charge of the Criminal Investigation Department of the Metropolitan Police, retired, and Henry was appointed to the post. He quickly established a Fingerprint Branch with three skilled officers from the former anthropometric office. They were Detective Inspector Charles Steadman (who headed the new service), Detective Sergeant Charles Stockley Collins – the star at Harry Jackson's trial – and Detective Constable Frederick Hunt.

Henry was personally involved in training these officers, aided by the collection he had brought from India. His men, in turn, travelled to prisons to instruct warders – Dr Garson had been sacked – to take prints on the new 'Henry forms'. As recommended by the Belper Committee, a far larger number of prisoners were now subject to identification procedures than in the days of the Troup system: anybody convicted of any of

UNIVERSITY OF WINCHESTER
LIBRARY

twenty-six offences and sentenced to more than a month's imprisonment was fingerprinted at the prison and the records forwarded for registration to the Central Office at New Scotland Yard. Among the new classes of crime that came under the purview of the identification service were arson, bankruptcy, embezzlement, forgery, housebreaking, indecent assault, sacrilege and unlawful possession.

Some prisoners, nevertheless, posed dilemmas. Suffragist prisoners at Holloway, for instance, were not initially fingerprinted ('because of the resistance such prisoners would no doubt offer'), but in 1913 the Commissioners of Prisons wrote to the Home Office seeking permission to photograph and fingerprint them. When Sylvia Pankhurst was in jail for 'default of finding sureties', the Home Office decided that she and others like her 'might properly be regarded as a "criminal prisoner" . . . and her finger prints taken'. By 1914, the number of offences for which fingerprinting was mandatory had risen sharply, including offences under the Official Secrets Act, 'conspiracies of all descriptions' and 'importuning male persons to commit unnatural offences'. Whilst the collection of prints grew, some 18,000 of the older anthropometric cards (which carried prints of the ten fingers for final identification) were reclassified by fingerprints. Five new officers had to be appointed to the Fingerprint Branch to cope with the additional work but the rewards were sweet indeed: 1,722 repeat offenders were identified by fingerprints during 1902, the first full year of operation, compared to 462 identifications in 1900, the last full year of operation of the combined system. By 1903, the number of identifications had risen to 3,642, about 70,000 fingerprint records were on file, and close to 350 records were being added weekly.

At last, the Commissioner felt confident enough to stop sending officers to Holloway Prison every week to look at remand prisoners in the hope of identifying recidivists. Fingerprints were not only identifying more recidivists but saving expensive police time. 'On a moderate computation', the Commissioner reported, 'the money value of the saving thus effected more than covers the cost of the establishment sanctioned for the working of the finger print system and all incidental expenses'. By the time the Commissioner, Sir Edward Bradford, wrote this, the fingerprint men had had their first taste of blood in court: that of Harry Jackson.

As fingerprinting triumphed, so did Edward Henry. When Sir Edward Bradford retired in 1903, the crown passed to Henry, who was to remain as Commissioner until 1918. Quite apart from fingerprinting, Henry pulled the Met to the technological cutting edge, introducing, for instance, telephones at police stations and typewriters at Scotland Yard, and did much to improve the average policeman's pay and service conditions. The Fingerprint Branch – independent since 1907 – was now overseen by Henry's successor as Assistant Commissioner, Melville Macnaghten, a champion of fingerprints, who, a decade earlier, had sat on the Troup Committee.

Macnaghten had earned another notable early success for fingerprinting by targeting racecourse thieves. A team of experts were sent to the Derby at Epsom and they took the prints of sixty thieves arrested there. Returning to the Central Office, they found records of previous conviction for twenty-seven of them. The next morning, a representative of the Yard was at court ready with the evidence. One prisoner, who denied all wrongdoing and 'assured the interrogating magistrate that he had never been in trouble before, and that a racecourse was, up to this time, an unknown world to him', was shown to be a man with ten previous convictions. 'Bless the fingerprints', the prisoner exclaimed. 'I knew they'd do me in!' The new technique struck such terror into the criminal heart that one old lag, on his way to prison – where he knew he would be fingerprinted and his past crimes discovered from the records – 'excoriated (with a pluck and perseverance worthy of a better cause) the papillary ridges of his thumbs and fingers by means a metal tag attached to his bootlace'. He successfully prevented his prints from being taken but the Yard was not to be outwitted. An expert was sent down, who, studying the lacerated fingers with a lens, managed to record the major distinguishing features of the patterns. Even that was unnecessary. Excoriation of the skin did not destroy the patterns of the ridges, which returned in pristine form once the skin had healed. All this crook could have achieved with his self-mutilation was a short delay of his identification. The Yard did not even allow him that small transient victory.

The next big test of fingerprinting came in May 1905, with the trial of the brothers Alfred and Albert Stratton at the Old Bailey for the murder of Thomas and Ann Farrow of Deptford. The victims, both nearly seventy, managed a shop in Deptford and were popular with neighbours. When their young shop assistant William Jones arrived for work on the morning of 27 March 1905, he found it closed, which had never happened before. Worried, he broke into the house to discover Thomas Farrow lying dead on the floor of the parlour – his head had been battered in. His wife was still alive but died a few days later in hospital. In the course of their investigations, the police found an empty cash box, with a print that could not be matched with the fingerprints of any of those involved in the case, including the deceased. A milkman and his assistant soon reported that they had seen two men leaving the shop in the early morning of the day of the murder. The strangers had slammed the door but it fell open – another witness later reported that he had seen it being shut by an old man, who seemed to be bleeding.

From evidence supplied by other witnesses, the suspicions of the police focused on two brothers, Albert and Alfred Stratton. Both were arrested and Detective Inspector Charles Collins of the Fingerprint Branch soon established that the thumb mark on the cash box was Alfred Stratton's.

The brothers were charged with homicide and tried at the Old Bailey in May 1905, where they pleaded not guilty. Richard Muir, again, prosecuted, and since the milkman and his boy could not identify the Stratton brothers as the men they had seen leaving the shop, the fingerprint evidence became absolutely crucial and it was up to Muir and Charles Collins to convince the jury of its reliability. Collins told the court about the system of fingerprint identification followed at the Yard, where they already had nearly 100,000 sets of prints in their collection. Although two or three similarities had been found between prints of different people, this was such a rare occurrence that there was no reason to doubt that fingerprints were unique to each individual. Since the print on the cash box (which Collins had photographed) matched the print of Alfred Stratton on twelve points, Collins had no doubt whatever that the two were identical. Enlarged photographs of the two prints were given to the jury and Collins demonstrated the technique of fingerprinting on a member of the jury.

The defence, rather rashly, argued that fingerprint evidence was unreliable. The defence witness on the issue was none other than Dr John G. Garson, lately of the Scotland Yard Anthropometric Office. Claiming ample experience with fingerprints, Garson declared that although the smudged cash-box print and the thumbprint of Alfred Stratton might just be identical, it was unlikely. At the very least, the prints were of two different fingers of the same individual. It came out during cross-examination that Garson, who no longer had any official access to police evidence, had offered to testify for the defence even before he had seen the photographs of the fingerprints. Muir then revealed that Garson had also written, at the same time, to the Public Prosecutor offering to be a prosecution witness.

The doctor mumbled that there was nothing irregular about his actions, since he was an independent witness, and the judge quipped: 'An absolutely untrustworthy one, I should think.' Garson averred that his evidence would not have differed whatever side he was on and the defence counsel battled on valiantly, denouncing fingerprint evidence as a dubious French import incompatible with British justice. The judge delivered a fair summing-up, pointing out that the cash-box print was made by perspiration – a 'latent' in modern jargon – and not an inked print like the one it was being compared to. The jury should not rely only on the evidence of the print, although the resemblances between the two were marked and should be counted as corroborative evidence against Alfred Stratton. After two hours of deliberation, the jury pronounced against the brothers, both of whom were sentenced to death.

Garson was not the only expert on the defence team. Although he did not appear on the witness stand, Henry Faulds had advised the defence and was present at the trial. Later, he argued in his *Guide to Finger-Print Identification* that the mark found on the cash box was so indistinct that it differed from the thumbprint of Alfred Stratton on at least as many points as it resembled it. If, as Scotland Yard seemed to think, four points of congruence were enough to pronounce a pair of prints as identical, then would the presence of 'four successive disagreements of pattern' permit a declaration of non-identity? 'A smudge of this quality', he concluded, 'should not be presented in court as evidence. The results are necessarily ambiguous or equivocal. It would be quite easy to find thousands of innocent men in whose finger patterns a few apparent coincidences could be read into such a hazy smudge'.

It was, in fact, the confession of one of the brothers in prison that finally reassured people that the technique was valid. Nevertheless, the guilty verdict robbed the already marginal Faulds of any significant audience. The trial of Harry Jackson had brought out all the strengths of the fingerprint system but it had not, of course, been sensational enough to grab public attention. The trial of the Deptford murderers, however, was tailor-made for publicity and fingerprints were now part of the national vocabulary. Without even mentioning the trial, which had taken place less than three months previously, the *Daily Express* began a 'finger-print competition' that ran weekly from July to September 1905. It was a murder mystery serial, specially written for the paper, each instalment of which was illustrated with the fingerprints of the characters.

The reader who successfully identified the murderer – who had obligingly left a print on the scene of crime, reproduced in the first instalment of the story – would win £100. (In order to guide its readers on the new technique, the newspaper commissioned a long article explaining the nature of fingerprint evidence in untechnical language from an expert 'who was most eminent among British authorities' and had 'long been identified with the science of identification by finger-prints'. This authority on fingerprinting was the recently humiliated Dr John Garson.) The final legal battle for the validity of fingerprint identification was won with the 1909 *Castleton* case, when the Criminal Appeal Court ruled that the court or a jury might accept 'the evidence of finger-prints though it be the sole ground of identification'. Fingerprinting was now home and dry.

The most piquant irony of this story is that from the north Bengal case onward, the history of fingerprinting followed a path first marked out – and partly explored – by Henry Faulds, the one man who had been completely excluded from the official history. It was Herschel, Galton and Henry who now formed what the historian George Wilton would later mockingly describe as the Fingerprint Triumvirate. At one level, this was simply because the history of fingerprinting was first authoritatively recounted by Francis Galton and no subsequent historical outline moved far beyond that account, except for

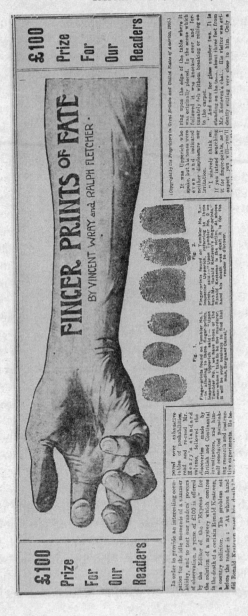

FIGURE 26

Fingerprinting in the media.

A competition in the *Daily Express* in the summer of the Deptford murder trial.

George Wilton's revisionist account of 1938, which argued passionately that it was Faulds who should be honoured as the founder of fingerprint identification. Until the end of his long life – he was to die at the age of 101 – the pugnacious Wilton kept up his battle with Scotland Yard and the government to win posthumous recognition for Faulds and a pension for his daughters but none of his efforts was to bear much fruit.

Why was Faulds marginalized? For Galton, it was not only Herschel's august lineage but also the unrivalled collection of evidence that were crucial. Faulds may have foreseen the future of fingerprinting far more clearly than Herschel or even Galton, but at no point in the early history of the technique did he *publish* sufficient evidence to demonstrate the persistence of fingerprint patterns through life – his experimental shaving-off of the ridges, only to watch them grow again was rightly dismissed by Galton, Herschel and others as insufficient in comparison with Herschel's collection of prints of the same individuals over decades. Secondly, Faulds could not produce a satisfactory classification scheme – although he claimed to have one – before the turn of the century, and by then the Henry system was already up and running.

Most of the factors that militated against Faulds were ultimately related to the Empire. Herschel's introduction of fingerprinting into the Registration Department and the jail at Hooghly was to provide Galton with some of his most valuable evidence. Faulds, a lone individual in Tokyo and then in England, simply never had that kind of administrative opportunity to try out the procedure; nor does he seem to have collected and preserved fingerprint specimens as extensively and meticulously as Herschel. A usable classification, of course, could have been evolved anywhere, at least in theory, but it so happened that it, too, was evolved at the heart of the Empire and had to be imported with its originator.

In its passage home, however, fingerprinting rapidly lost its imperial character. Fingerprinting in India had always been as important in civil situations as in the identification of criminals. Indeed, Herschel's only remotely criminological venture was to introduce it in the jail – and not to identify recidivists but to prevent the substitution of prisoners. Once Henry took it up, fingerprinting rapidly became central to police work but it was still used extensively in the civil domain, whether for registration, pensioner identification, or a variety of contractual matters unique to the Empire. When Henry came home with his technique, however, it was criminals alone (and initially, only recidivists, the most reprehensible of criminals) who came under its purview. The types of criminal subject to fingerprinting soon came to be extended but fingerprinting never really had an impact on non-criminal identification in England. As the judge Lord Atkin pointed out, 'we do not use finger-prints much on paper as merely a means of authenticating signatures. Most people can write their signature. The importance of finger-prints in this country is for the purpose of identifying the presence of individuals on the scene of a crime'. At the same gathering, the medical jurist and writer C. Ainsworth Mitchell suggested that the application of fingerprinting in civil matters had been prevented in England by 'the stigma which had become attached to the finger-print method of identification, through its exclusive use in criminal cases', a sentiment that, as we have seen, was echoed later by Karl Pearson in his biography of Galton.

Galton's vision of fingerprinting had been, like Herschel's, an imperial one: he was eager enough for fingerprinting to be used in crime, but above all he wanted it to be employed as a universal form of identification for the populace. Its need in the Empire for that purpose was, of course, greater because so many imperial subjects were illiterate, because coloured people were supposedly hard to distinguish and because they were so chronically dishonest, but Galton was emphatic that its use at home, too, would be beneficial in certain contexts. None of that ever happened. From the beginning until today, fingerprinting has been an exclusively criminological technique in Britain. It was Faulds' visionary proposal of 1880 that won out in Britain, but the process leading to that victory had originated in the radically different contexts, aims and presuppositions of colonial India. The fingerprint story was an Indian one – and there was hardly any room in it for a medical missionary who had once had a few interesting insights. As a Scotland Yard document opined after George Wilton had published his defence of Faulds' claim: 'Had he [Faulds] been wronged, as he believed, there was not much in it; but he was not wronged; and the world and its use of finger-prints would have gone on just the same had Faulds never lived. For the whole course of development was quite independent of him, and India was unaware even of its existence'. Nor were Faulds' chances of recognition by Scotland Yard improved by his alignment with the defence in one of the Yard's most crucial fingerprint cases. Nearly twenty years later, Charles Collins (now Superintendent Collins) remembered it clearly. 'I know very little of this individual', he scribbled on a 1921 file related to George Wilton's claims on behalf of Faulds. 'He was in the company of Dr Garson at the trial of the Strattons, and it was thought that he was to give evidence to back up Dr Garson'.

But why did fingerprint identification remain stubbornly confined to criminal identification in Britain? That was more than a matter of personalities. The British public, of course, has always been opposed to anything smacking of the idea of surveillance by the state. Only twice in recent history has that reluctance been overcome: during the two World Wars, when identity cards were issued for everybody and records kept of their addresses and other particulars. The measure was accepted as necessary – to help conscription, for instance, during the First World War – but was always found too 'Prussian'. The government had to discontinue the cards as soon as the wars were over, in spite of some members of the Civil Service being keen to persist with it. Even those short-lived identity cards, however, carried minimal information on them – nobody seems to have even raised the question of including fingerprints. Even in Argentina, where fingerprinting had been introduced very early in identifying immigrants and various marginal groups, the establishment of a general register of fingerprints in 1916 was soon declared unconstitutional, and all the fingerprints collected for it were destroyed. In Britain, no idea of a national register of fingerprints for all citizens was ever seriously considered. There was no exception to this rule, although an occasional civil servant was sometimes tempted by the possibilities in private. Charles Troup, for instance, wondered whether fingerprints should be used to identify the dead, especially mangled bodies in mine accidents. 'Of course', he observed in an 1895 letter to Francis Galton, 'this could only be possible if there were a general registration of the prints. It would be too like a sentence of death to require miners specially to record their marks'.

There were, however, two specific contexts where the government was willing to permit fingerprinting for purposes slightly broader than the identification of criminals by the police. The first was the army, where fingerprinting, it was believed, might be used to track deserters and nab fraudulent enlisters. A committee was formed in 1902 in the War Office, which interviewed, among others, various high military officials and Edward Henry. It was also the sole occasion when Henry Faulds was invited to present his views to the government – he used the opportunity to describe his own system of classification of prints but to no avail. Again, it was Henry who convinced the Committee that the easiest and most rapidly searchable classification of fingerprints was his. The military witnesses were unanimous that universal fingerprinting in the army would have a disastrous effect on enrolment. The Committee, therefore, recommended that although fingerprinting was an excellent means of identification, in the army, 'its application should be limited to men sentenced to imprisonment by Court-Martial or by Commanding Officer's award'. Fingerprinting, therefore, was rejected as a means of general identification of soldiers and introduced only for the military equivalent of criminals.

The one other area unrelated to standard police work where fingerprinting found a niche was in immigration control. From the 1890s, popular opinion in Britain was hardening against foreigners, especially Jews, who, it was believed, were entering the country in greater and greater numbers. The alien influx was seen as insanitary, a threat to jobs for the British population, and a huge source of criminals, prostitutes and anarchists, many of whom, to add insult to injury, claimed poor law relief. (Our own hysteria over asylum seekers and scrounging refugees has a venerable ancestry.) Fears of German and Jewish infiltration into Britain were rife – people were so exercised that a Royal Commission on Alien Immigration was appointed to investigate the matter. In its 1903 report, it pronounced that the current checks on immigration and the legislation against undesirable aliens were quite inadequate. In 1881, aliens resident in Britain had numbered 185,640; in 1901, the figure was 286,925. Violent crime committed by aliens was up: 28 cases in 1892, 58 in 1902. The Commission recommended that restrictions on the entry of aliens be imposed and the government responded with the Aliens Act of 1905. Charles Troup would later condemn this Act as 'from the administrative view one of the worst ever passed' but pass it did. Examples of categories of aliens to be excluded from Britain were prostitutes, people likely to 'become a charge on public funds' and 'persons of notoriously bad character'. Aliens convicted in court were subject to deportation orders. Aliens who landed in Britain in spite of refusal or those who did not leave after being served with an expulsion order were punishable with three months' penal servitude.

Any alien 'in whose case a Certificate has been given by a Court with a view to the making of an expulsion order under the Aliens Act, 1905, and who is confined in any prison . . . may be photographed and measured in the same way as a criminal prisoner', a government regulation decreed in February 1906. The 'measurements', of course, included fingerprinting. In February 1906, the Commissioner of the Metropolitan Police, Edward Henry, wrote to the Home Office that 'arrangements have been made at this Office for the reception and classification of the finger prints and records of expelled Aliens separately from the existing criminal records'. Even within the government, the measure was not accepted without demur. The Irish Under-Secretary enquired whether it was the government's intention that every alien in a prison, convicted or unconvicted, should be photographed and fingerprinted. Such a compulsory fingerprinting of an alien 'who is in no sense a criminal might', he pointed out, 'cause very great offence'. 'The unconvicted aliens under Certificates for Expulsion will be rare', a Home Office mandarin commented on this observation. 'The Irish government's tenderness for their feelings seems somewhat excessive. They were certainly intended to be included; and I doubt whether the technical objection has any weight'.

The official reply from the Home Office, however, was more careful in addressing the issue and found a saviour in the early imperial history of fingerprinting. The regulations certainly applied to unconvicted aliens, it was stressed, but 'there is nothing distinctively criminal about the taking of finger-prints which is merely a means of identification and is capable of being used for many other purposes than the recognition of criminals'. One looks in vain, however, for fingerprinting being used within Britain for any such purpose in 1906 or earlier. It was only in the Empire – that ultimate reservoir of aliens – where such uses had been and still were common. It was only when undesirable foreign elements came into Britain that the ideal of English liberty was suspended (and suspended only for those foreigners) and the original role of fingerprinting as 'merely a means of identification' – as opposed to a system only for 'the recognition of criminals' – was rediscovered.

Restrictions on aliens tightened severely over the twentieth century, especially from the time of the First World War. All aliens were now suspect and, along with passports, registration with the police became mandatory for most. The government acquired enormous powers to detain or expel aliens considered suspicious – on grounds not always spelt out in legislation. The Aliens Order of 1920, a legacy of wartime anxieties but retained and periodically amended up to 1948, allowed the police to 'take all such steps as may be reasonably necessary for photographing, measuring and otherwise identifying' all aliens in custody. Alien legislation in Britain has been too complicated and too ad hoc to permit too many generalizations. One point, however, is tolerably clear. Because of a range of circumstances – from war-fever and fear of revolution to frank racism – Britain, in the twentieth century, was no longer the haven for refugees, political activists and the poor and the unwashed that it had been in the middle years of the nineteenth century.

Nevertheless, as far as forms of *physical* surveillance were concerned, British governments have always been careful to avoid imposing them on all aliens. (Police registration of addresses and other particulars is the farthest that Britain has ever moved toward generalized identification of aliens.) When a Liverpool police officer wrote to the Home Office in 1920 to ask whether it would be permissible to take the fingerprints of applicants for naturalization and to send them to Scotland Yard for verification that the applicant was not a known criminal, the Superintendent of the Metropolitan Police Special Branch advised the government that although such a procedure 'would supply definite information as to whether a person had been convicted or not of a serious offence . . . it is fairly certain that the majority of applicants would resent the proposal and perhaps refuse to submit themselves to such procedure'. A civil servant observed that to make fingerprinting 'part of the routine of enquiry into every applicant, though a laudable suggestion, seems to be slightly oppressive and would certainly be resented by the more respectable applicants'. Another warned that the Liverpool police would 'stir up a hornet's nest' if they attempted this scheme. The Home Secretary decided, unsurprisingly, that 'the thorough investigation which is already made is a sufficient safeguard'. Even foreigners – as long as they were respectable by the standards of the era – had some rights in England: fingerprinting them even if only to verify their innocence was unacceptable. Compare this with the French attempt in 1888 to identify every resident foreigner by anthropometry. This initiative was actually defeated by practical difficulties but the 1912 directive that every resident without a fixed address should carry an anthropometric identity card was more successful. Such measures were never considered in Britain and even in its colonies, only certain groups – such as the criminal tribes in India – were subjected to similar surveillance.

And, of course, subjecting the British national to fingerprinting, no matter for how laudable or harmless a motive, was – and is – anathema. In 1937, when an MP asked the government to consider establishing a national register of fingerprints to help in identifying, among others, unidentified people suffering from loss of memory or reason, the Home Secretary stated in a written reply that while he agreed that fingerprints 'undoubtedly afford an easy and certain means of establishing identity', he 'would not feel justified in considering the question of a national finger print registry . . . unless he were satisfied that there is a real and general desire for such a system'. Later that year, the

Secretary of State for Foreign Affairs was asked by the same Member whether he would order the inclusion of 'alongside the signature, the print of the right thumb of the holder of the passport'. 'Apart from the objection which exists in the mind of the public to any requirement of fingerprints', the Rt Hon Robert Anthony Eden replied, there were many 'insurmountable difficulties' to instituting such a requirement and he was unconvinced that 'any substantial public benefit would accrue from its adoption'. The MP then informed the Secretary of State that a recent International Police Congress had recommended the inclusion of fingerprints on passports to prevent forgery and suggested 'that it is only prejudice which stands in the way of adoption of a practice which would prove to be a very sound one'. A rather exasperated Eden thanked the Honourable Member for this information but declared that 'life is complicated enough already'. Another MP quipped, 'Will the right hon. Gentleman consider instituting this system for police officers first as an experiment?'

Herschel and his admirers had thought of fingerprinting as a general, universal system of identification, while Henry Faulds, who had also begun with expansive notions of the applicability of fingerprints, had soon come to focus exclusively on the detection of criminals. Although Faulds's ideas were never to be taken seriously in Britain, the *form* in which fingerprinting was adopted at home – as a means of identifying criminals alone – was essentially the same as what the Scottish doctor and missionary had urged for so many years with such fruitless passion. His name was excluded from the official history but it was he whose idea had won in Britain, not Herschel's or even Galton's. In a parable by the Argentine writer Jorge Luis Borges, two theologians engage in a fight to the death on doctrinal minutiae; when they reach heaven, however, their differences matter so little to the Almighty that He regards them as identical. The struggle of Faulds and Herschel was, no doubt, less exalted in its setting but the irony of its outcome was quintessentially Borgesian.

Things, however, seem to be changing. If one looks at immigration control, then fingerprinting is no longer a purely criminological procedure in Britain. The Asylum and Immigration Appeals Act of 1993, for instance, provided for the fingerprinting of *all* asylum seekers – not simply the expelled aliens targeted by the 1905 Aliens Act – and of their dependants. Refusal to comply entailed arrest without warrant and forcible fingerprinting. The Immigration and Asylum Act of 1999 extended fingerprinting to anybody arriving in the UK without a valid passport and to various other kinds of immigration offenders. In early 2002, the government announced that henceforth, asylum seekers would be issued with 'smart cards' carrying their fingerprints, photographs and details about their age and nationality. The cards would also carry some data that would be accessible only to authorized immigration officials. Such smart cards might also be introduced as 'entitlement cards' for all citizens, which, the Home Secretary feels, would help combat benefit fraud, tax evasion and the employment of illegal immigrants. Even more recently, the head of the UK Passport Service has suggested that these cards be loaded with identity markers such as iris scans or fingerprints and used as 'smart passports'. It has also been rumoured that the Home Secretary is considering the use of an online database of fingerprints to determine the first member country of the European Union visited by an asylum seeker. (European Union regulations stipulate that applications for asylum must be made at the first member country visited by the applicant. Hence, if somebody seeking asylum in Britain can be shown to have come here via, say, France, then he can be returned to France without any further investigation of his claim.)

The initiatives that have actually been implemented, harsh as they are, continue to be aimed, however, at a group that has been a problem for British governments since the end of the nineteenth century, rather than at foreigners in general or even at all members of any particular racial group. For all the racial anxieties that have animated debates over immigration and encouraged the passage of ever stricter laws, these laws have left the dirty job of racial exclusion to civil servants immune from parliamentary scrutiny. As Sir Alec Douglas-Home, Secretary of State for Commonwealth Relations, wrote in 1955, it was 'politically impossible to legislate for a colour bar' and nobody, in any case, wanted 'to keep out immigrants of good type'. The solution, the Home Office proposed, was to exercise non-legislative controls through immigration officers, who 'could, without giving rise to trouble or publicity, exercise such a measure of discrimination as we think desirable'. Long before 1955 and long after, British legislation on aliens was guided by this tradition. Legislation was more liberal than the actual, ground-level procedures of immigration control. Surveillance by techniques such as fingerprinting, however, needs legislative authority. Not surprisingly, therefore, it has been confined only to categories defined by offence, rather than by race, and the alien, once admitted to the country and allowed to work, has never been subject to any surveillance other than police registration. (And even there, one encounters startling exceptions. Currently, European Union citizens, of course, do not need to register with the police to live here, nor to have work permits to accept a job. Commonwealth citizens do need work permits but are exempt from registration. The citizens of Britain's great political ally America, however, need work permits *and* have to register with the police. Whatever might explain the phenomenon of Indians, Pakistanis or Nigerians being exempt from police surveillance while Americans, regardless of colour, stand in long queues with Turks, Russians and Brazilians at alien registration offices, it is unlikely to be racism.)

So much for aliens. What, however, of British subjects? Their lives are now an open book to the state and its innumerable agencies. But not their bodies. For all its growing nosiness into lives, finances and personal affairs, the government has not so far touched the average law-abiding subject – or, for that matter, the average law-abiding foreigner – with any technique of *physical* surveillance, whether anthropometry or fingerprinting or iris scans. Obviously, the new 'entitlement cards' or the 'smart passports' could breach that barrier if they were introduced and if they actually carried fingerprints or other markers of bodily identity. The British state would then have crossed the Rubicon of the body. And that is the point when English liberty will die.

CONCLUSION

Home, Empire, Liberty

Britain's impact on her colonies, it is scarcely necessary to state, was fundamental, wide ranging and long lasting. Historians are only beginning to appreciate, however, that the influence of Empire on the mother country was far from negligible. There is no better instance of this intimate, reciprocal interaction of home and Empire than the history of fingerprinting in colonial India and its transmission to Britain. As Lord Riddell, President of the Medico-Legal Society in London, observed, 'Whether Empire Free Trade in foods is possible I do not know, but we have Free Trade in ideas within the Empire. It is interesting to know that, owing to the requirements of India, learned men . . . developed this wonderful system of finger-prints which has been found to be most useful in this and other civilised countries. This is another benefit conferred by the British on mankind'. ('Unhappily', he added, 'we are such a modest nation that we never advertise all we have done'.)

Now that we have looked in some detail at the development of fingerprinting in British India, it is time to look deeper into the conditions that encouraged and sustained it. And here we confront the central paradox of Britain's rule in India. In the nineteenth century, at the height of the Raj, Britain was a nation unflinching in its commitment to liberalism, whether to the unrestricted liberty of the trader or to the unfettered personal liberty of the English subject. And yet, in its largest colonial dependency, the rule of Britain was explicitly, unabashedly despotic. As James Fitzjames Stephen put it with a stark honesty rare at the time, Britain's authority in India stemmed from conquest, not consent. An Indian subject of Queen Victoria or King Edward VII might possess many things, but not the liberty guaranteed to a British subject. Even the sacred dogma of free trade applied only to the cotton mills of Lancashire selling textiles to India and to the export of cotton fibre from India to Lancashire. The Indian trader or entrepreneur eager to spin the local cotton and sell it in the local market, however, was unacceptable. Laissez-faire was all very well for home but it did not, as Eric Hobsbawm has pointed out, apply to India. Even John Stuart Mill, the author of *On Liberty*, that luminous plea for individual freedom, emphasized that only 'human beings in the maturity of their faculties' had a right to liberty. Children did not; nor did those who could not take adequate care of themselves. 'For the same reason', added Mill, 'we may leave out of consideration those backward states of society in which the race itself may be considered as in its nonage'. Mill, an employee for many years of the East India Company, had elsewhere defined the Indian character as 'passive and slavish' and scholars have often wondered at his inability to apply his own liberal credo to the government of India and other British dependencies. Surprising as it may be, however, this arch-liberal of the nineteenth century was unambiguous in his declaration that 'despotism is a legitimate mode of government in dealing with barbarians, provided the end be their improvement'.

Race, in the narrower sense, was only one factor in this larger despotic approach. Indians were to be ruled without consent not because they had dark skins but because they were inferior in *every* way. Culturally in thrall to caste, historically ruled by fierce tyrants from virtually the dawn of time, spiritually lacking in any concept of liberty, superstitious in religion, mendacious by nature and slavishly ingratiating in disposition,

Indians were neither deserving nor, indeed, desirous of democratic rule. It was this absence of personal liberty in India – and the distrust of the native's word and his bond – that enabled as well as encouraged the application of sophisticated identification techniques on an unimaginably wider scale than in Britain itself. Anthropometry, for instance, was a valued technique in Britain but compare how Thurston collected his data at his museum in Madras with Francis Galton's collection of similar data in South Kensington. In Madras, one could jump on people with goniometers; in London, one could only seek voluntary experimental subjects. As for Herschel's approach to fingerprinting, it evolved from a vague unease about the honesty of a contractor and matured into a *compulsory* signature not just for criminals but for perfectly ordinary people, whether executants of deeds, indentured labourers or pensioners. In Britain, however, in spite of opportunities for its civil use being pointed out by Francis Galton as well as by a Member of Parliament, fingerprint identification was compulsory only for criminals and, at most, for undesirable aliens. To repeat, the body of the freeborn English subject was untouchable as long as he had not demonstrably infringed the laws of the realm. The body of the colonial subject, however, was another matter altogether.

George Wilton was on the right track when, contemplating the British refusal to use fingerprinting for general identification of the populace, he remarked that 'British people seem . . . reluctant to apply methods suited, as many probably think, to dark and more or less primitive races'. It was, however, more than a matter of mere racism, and the racist beliefs of individual progenitors of fingerprinting played no uniform, predictable role in the genesis of the technique. Galton may have been a racist in our terms; Herschel's racial suspicions of Indians were indubitably important in motivating his work on identification but those suspicions did not interfere with his dispensation of impartial justice; and in none of the writings and private correspondence of Edward Henry have I ever encountered a single remark on the indistinguishability of Indian features or even on the venerable theme of the innate duplicity of Indians. The emergence of fingerprinting in British India, in short, was often influenced by racial beliefs but far more important than that racism was the fundamental character of British rule in India.

British dominion over India was mighty at one level and strangely insecure in others. Unquestioned authority went hand in hand with pervasive fears of being deceived by the populace. After the Mutiny of 1857, these fears intensified. It is this curious combination of despotic rule and intense insecurity that is the ultimate explanation of the origin of systematic fingerprinting in the Raj as well as of the astonishing extent of its application. Only in India could it be done on that scale and only in India did the British feel the *need* to do it on that scale. Problems of identification were, of course, seen as important even in nineteenth-century Britain – but only for relatively well-demarcated groups that had already forfeited their liberty. And only such subhuman denizens of the sceptr'd isle would ever be subjected to fingerprinting. The child of the illiberal Empire, immediately upon arrival in liberal England, lost the untrammelled liberty and power it had enjoyed in the tropics. Thrust into the dungeons of the British state and entrusted with the guardianship of its least worthy subjects, it was to languish there permanently, a captivity from which nobody, not even Sir Francis Galton, could secure its release.

APPENDIX

The Classification of Fingerprints: From Galton to Henry

Although this book is not concerned with the technicalities of fingerprint identification and classification, so much of the history of fingerprinting has turned upon the issue of classification that readers might appreciate a brief overview of the major problems and their ultimate resolution.

Although quickly convinced of the value of fingerprints in identification, Francis Galton realized that the very diversity of patterns which made them unique identifiers ensured that one could not easily divide all fingerprints into a few clearly defined categories. 'A complex pattern', he observed, 'is capable of suggesting various readings, as the figuring on a wall-paper may suggest a variety of forms and faces to those who have such fancies'. Different prints from the same finger could deceive the eye, especially when focusing on the pattern as a whole. Such errors could be avoided only by fixing on 'a well-defined point or points of reference in the patterns'. What could serve as these points? The whole palm and all the fingers were covered with ridges but the ridges ran roughly parallel to each other on the fingers until they approached the tips, where, the fingernail

disturbs their parallelism and squeezes them downwards on both sides of the finger. Consequently, the ridges that run close to the tip are greatly arched, those that successively follow are gradually less arched until, in some cases, all signs of the arch disappear at about the level of the first joint.

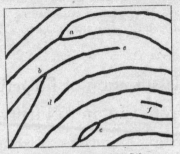

Characteristic peculiarities in Ridges
(about 8 times the natural size).

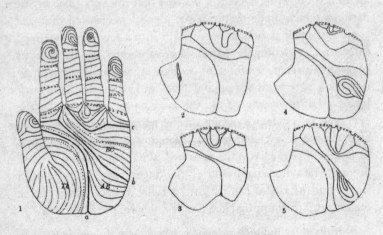

Systems of Ridges, and the Creases in the Palm.

FIGURE 27

Francis Galton's attempts to explain different fingerprint patterns.

Usually, however, this gradual transition from an arch to a straight line fails to be carried out, causing a break in the orderly sequence, and a consequent interspace.

And within this interspace one could find 'an independent system of ridges arranged in loops or in scrolls, and this interpolated system forms the "pattern"'. If one drew a line to connect the spots on the sides of the fingers from where the ridges began to diverge to form the interspace, it could serve as the 'base line whereby the pattern may be oriented, and the position of any point roughly charted'. The pattern within the interspace should then be studied with a lens of moderate magnifying power – a very powerful lens narrowed the field of view far too much – and outlined on the print by pen.

A carefully traced outline immediately converted the print into an intelligible pattern. 'What seemed before to be a vague and bewildering maze of lineations over which the glance wandered distractedly, seeking in vain for a point on which to fix itself, now suddenly assumes the shape of a sharply-defined figure.' With sufficient practice, the eye learnt to trace outlines by habit and it proved unnecessary to actually trace one on the print.

The predominant patterns found in all fingerprints were the arch, the loop and the whorl. These could serve as the starting-point for a classificatory scheme. 'The Arch-Loop-Whorl, or more briefly, the A.L.W. system of classification', Galton remarked,

> while in some degree artificial, is very serviceable for preliminary statistics ... A minute subdivision under numerous heads would necessitate a proportional and somewhat overwhelming amount of statistical labour. Fifty-four different standard varieties are by no means an extravagant number, but to treat fifty-four as thoroughly as three would require eighteen times as much material and labour. Effort is economised by obtaining broad results from a discussion of the

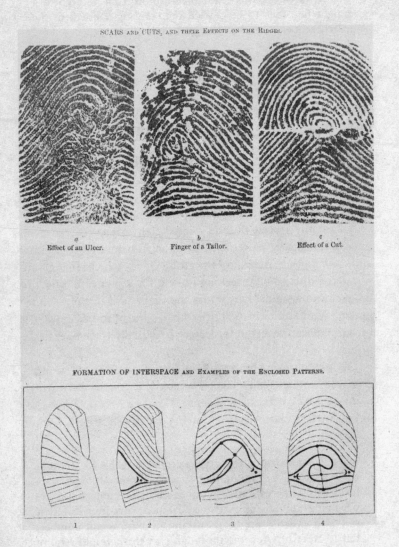

SCARS AND CUTS, AND THEIR EFFECTS ON THE RIDGES.

a   *b*   *c*
Effect of an Ulcer.   Finger of a Tailor.   Effect of a Cut.

FORMATION OF INTERSPACE AND EXAMPLES OF THE ENCLOSED PATTERNS.

1   2   3   4

FIGURE 28

The patterns within patterns in the ridges on the fingers.

EXAMPLES OF OUTLINED PATTERNS
(The Specimens are rolled impressions of natural size).

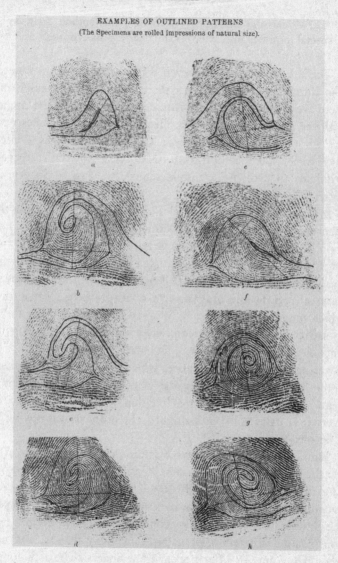

FIGURE 29
How to outline patterns.

A.L.W. classes, afterwards verifying or extending them by special inquiries into a few of the further subdivisions.

The A.L.W. scheme, however, was a very rough one indeed. The three categories were anything but separate entities and there were innumerable transitional forms linking the arches with the loops, the loops with the whorls, and the arches with the whorls. Galton called these 'compound' patterns – later, they were called composites – and these posed the biggest problems to evolving a simple scheme to classify fingerprint patterns.

In 1920, the scientist Ethel Elderton, in her study of the inheritance of fingerprint patterns, recalled that Galton had soon realized that for a truly precise and scientific study of fingerprints, one had to differentiate every 'mixed' pattern. And this was virtually impossible. All that could be achieved was to lump all prints into four or five relatively broad categories, which might suffice for criminological identification but failed to satisfy the more exact requirements of science. 'There is no difficulty', Elderton explained, 'in making 53 or more groups of finger-prints; the difficulty arises when we have to agree where arches end and loops begin and where loops end and whorls begin'. Since transitional cases like that occurred about once in every four pairs of hands examined, the problem was obviously a serious one.

But Galton's system of classification proved inadequate even for the humbler task of criminal identification. He went all out to evolve a more rough-and-ready lexicon that might serve for everyday identification. The basic principle was fairly simple: the different classes in the lexicon 'should depend upon a few conspicuous differences of patterns in many fingers, and not upon many minute differences in a few fingers'. The arch–loop–whorl division seemed to offer the best scheme and although one could, of course, differ about how many fingers to use for the index, Galton preferred to use all ten. (Herschel had never stipulated any rule and was inconsistent in his own practice but Faulds had always recommended using prints from all ten fingers.) Galton grouped the ten digits in four groups: A (fore, middle and ring fingers of the right hand), B (fore, middle and ring fingers of the left hand), C (thumb and little finger of right hand) and D (thumb and little finger of the left hand). Using 'a', 'l' and 'w' to indicate arch, loop and whorl, the prints of ten fingers could be reduced into four sets of notations, which could be arranged alphabetically in an index. A specimen index entry on this scheme might be as follows:

A	B	C	D
lal	aaw	ll	ll

The loop pattern, when found on the forefingers, was further divided into 'i' and 'o' forms according to whether the loop sloped toward the thumb (*i*nward) or toward the little finger (*o*utward). Later, these would come to be called 'r' and 'u' (for *r*adial and *u*lnar, from the two bones of the forearm they were directed toward). Incorporating this in the index, the specimen entry above could read as follows:

A	B	C	D
ial	aaw	ll	ll

Loops found on the other fingers were not divided into 'i' and 'o' subtypes because Galton soon found that apart from the inner-directed slope being rare on the other fingers, taking all slopes into account was inadvisable: 'The judgment became fatigued and the eye puzzled by having to assign opposite meanings to the same actual direction of a slope in the right and left hands respectively'. Galton continued for some years to tinker with this classification, making major and minor changes. Within limits, it worked well but the transitional cases continued to be an insuperable problem.

There was another issue that posed a problem. Since certain patterns occurred more frequently than others, a formula such as *oll, oll, ll, ll* could apply to as many as 6 per cent of a sample of cases. In a large collection, such duplication would make searching quite impracticable by swelling some categories into an unmanageable bulk. Galton did try to develop a scheme of subclassification to differentiate such identical patterns but this was far too complicated for the average policeman who would have to use it.

As we saw earlier, Edward Henry (or, if the unsubstantiated claims are to be trusted, his Indian subordinate Azizul Haque) began with Galton's basic division of ridge patterns into arches, loops and whorls, but added a fourth type called composites. As the name suggests, a composite was a print which combined features of more than one of the three Galtonian patterns. After the prints had been taken, their patterns were recorded in pairs, beginning with the right thumb and right index fingers and ending with the left ring and left little finger. It had been found that approximately 5 per cent of all patterns were arches, 60 per cent were loops and 35 per cent were whorls and composites. Henry's primary classification, therefore, subsumed the smaller category of arches into the far bigger one of loops, and the composites were included with the whorls. Using this scheme, one could spell out *all* possible combinations of patterns for a pair of digits.

To use Henry's own example, the right thumb and the right index finger could both be loops, the thumb could be a loop and the index finger a whorl or vice versa, or both could be whorls. Each pair of digits could exhibit any of these combinations but no more. The possible combinations for each pair of digits was Loop/Loop, Loop/Whorl, Whorl/Loop or Whorl/Whorl, the numerator signifying the thumb or the first digit of each pair, and the denominator the index finger or the second of the pair. For two pairs of digits taken *together*, any of the possible patterns of each pair could, of course, be combined with any of those possible for the second pair: the total number of possible combinations for two pairs was, therefore, 16. For *three* pairs of digits *together*, there were 64 possible combinations; for four pairs together, there were 256, and for all five pairs of digits, 1,024. The number of possible combinations, in other words, was quadrupled with the addition of each pair of digits: 4 for one pair, 16 for two, 64 for three, 256 for four and 1,024 for all five. Since 1,024 was the square of thirty-two, 'a cabinet containing thirty-two sets of thirty-two pigeon-holes arranged horizontally would provide locations for all combinations of Loops and Whorls of the ten digits taken in pairs'. The arrangement of the cards in the pigeonholes and the procedure for searching it are explained in the illustration (see Figure 22, p. 142) but as Henry pointed out, a cabinet or even pigeonholes were not essential. The cards (which weren't necessary either – one could use slips of paper) could simply be filed as separate bundles according to the denominator of the primary classification.

Later, it was found – again, according to the alternative account, by Azizul Haque – that the key required to search the cabinet could be replaced by a fairly simple mathematical formula. Again, one began with pairs of fingers and classifying all patterns as either loops or whorls, yielding, say, the combinations L/W, W/L, L/L, W/W, L/W. Now, numbers were assigned to the whorls: a whorl in the first pair was 16, 8 in the second, 4 in the third, 2 in the fourth and 1 in the fifth. Loops got no numbers. On this scheme, the combination of the example became 0/16, 8/0, 0/0, 2/2 and 0/1. The top and bottom figures of the individual fractions were added up, giving, in this case, the total 10/19. Since the rows and pigeonholes were numbered from 1 to 32, not from 0 to 31, 1 was added to the figures, giving 11/20. This fraction was then inverted, giving 20/11, which was the primary classification number. The prints, in this case, would be located in the twentieth pigeonhole of the eleventh horizontal row of the cabinet. Although there were 1,024 possible combinations, the classification numbers ranged only between 1 and 32, the number of pigeonholes in each row of the cabinet.

With this scheme, certain combinations, being more frequent, became far too large for easy searching – a secondary classification was, therefore, essential. The details need not detain us but the hitherto excluded arches and composite patterns now came into play – loops were now divided, for instance, into arches, tented arches and radial (inner) and ulnar (outer) loops. The formula obtained at the end of the secondary classification was, again, a fraction such as

$$\frac{1 \ aAr}{1 \ rRa}$$

This formula (in which the top figures referred to the right fingers and the lower ones to the left) would tell the classifier that the combination in question was located in the first pigeonhole of the first row and in the sub-group characterized by an arch on the right thumb and on the right index finger and an inner (radial) loop on one finger of the right hand and inner (radial) loops on the left thumb and index finger and an arch on one of the fingers of the left hand.

Here is one example of how the system worked. The first pigeonhole of the cabinet (1/1) contained *all* cards with impressions that were *all* loops. Since loops were divisible into the subtypes listed earlier (including arches) and they could, of course, occur in different combinations, there were nine subclasses within the pigeonhole 1/1:

Subclass A/A: Arches on left and right index fingers
Subclass A/R: Arch on the right and inner (radial) loop on the left index finger

File	Subfile	Group	File	Subfile	Group	File	Subfile	Group
1/1	A/A		1/1	A/A				
„	„	$\frac{Aa}{aA2a}$	„	„	$\frac{aA2a}{aA3a}$			
„	„	$\frac{aAa}{aA2a}$	„	„	$\frac{A3a}{aA3a}$			
„	„	$\frac{A2a}{aA2a}$	„	„	$\frac{aA3a}{aA3a}$	1/1	U/U	
„	„	$\frac{aA2a}{A3a}$	1/1	R/A	$\frac{R}{A}$			
„	„	$\frac{aA2a}{aA3a}$			$\frac{aR}{A}$			
„	„	$\frac{aA2a}{A}$			$\frac{Ra}{A}$			
„	„	$\frac{A3a}{aA}$						
„	„	$\frac{A3a}{Aa}$			And so on, repre-			
„	„	$\frac{A3a}{aAa}$			senting 64 groups,			
„	„	$\frac{A3a}{A2a}$			corresponding to			
„	„	$\frac{A3a}{aA2a}$			those of $\frac{1}{1}\ \frac{A}{A}$			
„	„	$\frac{A3a}{A3a}$						
„	„	$\frac{aA3a}{A}$	1/1	U/A				
„	„	$\frac{aA3a}{aA}$	1/1	A/R				
„	„	$\frac{aA3a}{Aa}$	1/1	R/R	Each having 64 groups, corresponding			
„	„	$\frac{aA3a}{aAa}$	1/1	R/U	to those of $\frac{1}{1}\ \frac{A}{A}$			
„	„	$\frac{aA3a}{A2a}$	1/1	U/R				
			1/1	A/U				
			1/1	R/U				

Subfile $\frac{1}{1}\ \frac{U}{U}$ forms two Subfiles, viz.: $\frac{1}{1}\ \frac{U}{U}$ (lettered), in which, though both index fingers are ulnar Loops, some of the other digits are Arches or Radials, and Subfile $\frac{1}{1}\ \frac{U}{U}$, in which all the digits are ulnar Loops. For details see next page.

FIGURE 30

Some of the categories of Edward Henry's
classification of fingerprints.

Subclass R/A: Reverse of A/R

Subclass R/R: Inner (radial) loop on left and right index fingers

Subclass A/U: Arch on the right and outer (ulnar) loop on the left index finger

Subclass U/A: Reverse of above

Subclass R/U: Inner (radial) loop on right and outer (ulnar) loop on left index finger

Subclass U/R: Reverse of above

Subclass U/U: Outer (ulnar) loop on both index fingers

All these subclasses were further divided according to various criteria: the subclass A/A could, for instance, be differentiated into 256 separate groups. In practice, however, a smaller number of 64 sufficed. The system was extraordinarily thorough in allowing for all possibilities: if one finger was missing, for example, the classification was made according to the pattern on the other hand. If the same digit was missing on both hands, their impressions were assumed to be whorls.

Those complex subdivisions, however, do not seem to have hindered the ease with which the database could be searched. There was no longer any reason not to use fingerprints as the sole markers of the identity of individuals. It was, as we have seen, the unavailability of a usable classification that had prevented the Troup Committee from recommending the exclusive use of fingerprints for the identification of criminals. About six years later, however, such a classification was available and the Belper Committee did not hesitate, in spite of objections from some of its witnesses, to recommend the replacement of anthropometric identification by fingerprinting.

Further Reading

Not too many histories of criminal identification are available for the general reader, although many specialist studies exist. The aim of the following survey is not to provide an exhaustive bibliography but simply to indicate the range of material available. Needless to say, I have used these works as sources and drawn extensively upon many of them. If this were an academic work, one could acknowledge these debts in footnote after footnote but in the absence of that handy device, this statement and the following citations must serve to indicate my gratitude.

The best works to start with are Simon Cole, *Suspect Identities: A History of Fingerprinting and Criminal Identification* (Cambridge, Mass.: Harvard University Press, 2001); and an essay by the same author, 'What Counts for Identity? The Historical Origins of the Methodology of Latent Fingerprint Identification', *Science in Context*, 12 (1999): 139–72. Ronald R. Thomas, in his *Detective Fiction and the Rise of Forensic Science* (Cambridge: Cambridge University Press, 1999), shows how the evolution of criminology and crime fiction proceeded hand in hand in the nineteenth century and deals with, inter alia, the development of fingerprint identification. Two other works are indispensable for comprehending the deeper character and the many nuances of the nineteenth-century interest in identification: Carlo Ginzburg, 'Morelli, Freud and Sherlock Holmes: Clues and Scientific Method', translated by Anna

Davin, *History Workshop Journal*, 9 (Spring 1980): 5–36 and Michel Foucault, *Discipline and Punish: The Birth of the Prison*, trans. Alan Sheridan (London: Penguin, 1991). The collection of essays edited by Jane Caplan and John Torpey, *Documenting Individual Identity: The Development of State Practices in the Modern World* (Princeton, NJ: Princeton University Press, 2001) is also strongly recommended.

On Bertillon, Henry T. F. Rhodes's biography, *Alphonse Bertillon: Father of Scientific Detection* (London: Harrap, 1956) is a good place to start (although it tends to be hagiographical) but should be supplemented by Alain Corbin's splendid, wide-ranging essay on nineteenth-century concerns with individual identity, 'Backstage', in *A History of Private Life*, vol. 4, edited by Michelle Perrot (Cambridge, Mass.: Harvard University Press, 1990), pp. 451–667. Bertillon's system is spelt out in *Signaletic Instructions including the Theory and Practice of Anthropometrical Identification*, edited by R. W. McClaughry (Chicago: Werner, 1896), a translation of Bertillon's *Signalements anthropometriques*.

For fingerprints as for Bertillonage, Cole's *Suspect Identities* is the most comprehensive study but George Wilton's treatise, *Fingerprints: History, Law and Romance* (London: Hodge, 1938) remains indispensable for its wealth of material, and Gerald Lambourne, *The Fingerprint Story* (London: Harrap, 1984) is well worth reading. Colin Beavan, *Fingerprints: The Origins of Crime Detection and the Murder Case that Launched Forensic Science* (New York: Hyperion, 2001), although generally rather a sketchy account, is fairly informative on the Deptford murder trial.

On Henry Faulds, Wilton's *Fingerprints* is still the richest source, although Beavan offers some fresh material. Of Faulds's own works, two of the most important are *Guide to Finger-Print Identification* (Hanley: Wood, Mitchell, 1905) and *Dactylography, or the Study of Finger-Prints* (Halifax: Milner, 1912). His first, historic publication on fingerprinting was 'On the Skin-furrows of the Hand', *Nature*, 22 (1880): 605. For samples of his assaults on Herschel, see 'On the Identification of Habitual Criminals by Finger-Prints', *Nature*, 50 (1894): 548; and 'The Permanence of Finger-Print Patterns', *Nature*, 98 (1917): 388.

For Herschel's retrospective accounts of his 'discovery', see his 'Skin Furrows of the Hand', *Nature*, 23 (1880): 76; 'Finger-Prints', *Nature*, 51 (1894): 77–8; 'The Discovery of Finger-Prints', *The Times*, 26 January 1909: 4, col. D; and *Origin of Finger-Printing* (London: Oxford University Press, 1916). There is no biography but much information is available in Eileen Shorland, 'Sir William James Herschel and the Birth of Finger-print Identification', *Library Chronicle (University of Texas)*, NS 14 (1980): 25–33. The world of colonial administration in Herschel's time is brought to life in Henry Cotton, *Indian and Home Memories* (London: Unwin, 1911), which is also informative on Herschel's early experimentation with fingerprinting. Indispensable to understanding the impetus for Herschel's work is Blair B. Kling, *The Blue Mutiny: The Indigo Disturbances in Bengal 1859–1862* (Philadelphia: University of Pennsylvania Press, 1966). The *Report of the Indigo Commission* is available in *House of Commons Parliamentary Papers*, 44 (1861): 335 et seq. (Herschel's evidence: pp. 568–74). Herschel's private papers and correspondence on fingerprinting are at the Bancroft Library, University of California at Berkeley (BANC MSS 92/630z); some important letters on the subject are in the Galton Papers at University College London. Administrative papers related to his work in India (but not to fingerprinting) are available in the Oriental and India Office Collections of the British Library (MSS Eur D 860).

On Francis Galton, only the doughtiest readers would wish to tackle Karl Pearson's massive biography *The Life, Letters and Labours of Francis Galton*, 3 vols in 4 (Cambridge: Cambridge University Press, 1914–30) but the long section (vol. 3A:

138–216) on Galton's work on personal identification contains much of interest on fingerprints. Compact alternatives are D. W. Forrest, *Francis Galton: The Life and Work of a Victorian Genius* (London: Elek, 1974) and Nicholas W. Gillham, *A Life of Sir Francis Galton* (Oxford: Oxford University Press, 2001). Francis Galton, *Finger Prints* (London: Macmillan, 1892), *Decipherment of Blurred Finger-Prints (Supplementary Chapter to Finger Prints)* (London: Macmillan, 1893) and *Finger Print Directories* (London: Macmillan, 1895) contain virtually all of Galton's thoughts on the subject, to which he added little in his autobiography, *Memories of My Life* (London: Methuen, 1909). Galton's research notes, collections of fingerprints, and correspondence with, among others, Herschel and Henry are at the Manuscripts and Rare Book Room at University College London Library.

Edward Henry's system of fingerprint classification and brief remarks on its origins are available in his *Classification and Uses of Finger Prints* (1st edition, London: HMSO, 1900; many subsequent editions up to 1937). B. C. Bridges, *Practical Fingerprinting* (New York: Funk & Wagnalls, 1942) provides further details on the Henry system as well as on other schemes of fingerprint classification. John Rowland's *The Finger-Print Man: The Story of Sir Edward Henry* (London: Lutterworth Press, 1959), although written with the cooperation of Henry's daughters, is not, in the author's own words, 'a formal biography' but 'an imaginative tale' – it should, therefore, be used with the greatest caution. Maurice Garvie's video biography of Henry is not publicly available but the gist of his research can be obtained from his article, 'The Life and Times of Sir Edward Henry', in the *International Criminal Police Review*, no. 480 (2000): 24–31. The location of his private papers is unknown, although some important letters are available in the Galton Papers and the Herschel Papers at Berkeley. Official papers related to his career at Scotland Yard are at the Public Record

Office but they are closed until 2032 – his reports as the Inspector General of the Bengal Police, however, are available at the Oriental and India Office Collections of the British Library (IOR V/24/3202). Some interesting details on the early days of fingerprinting at the Yard are available in Melville L. Macnaghten, *Days of My Years* (London: Edward Arnold, 1914) and, for a later period, in Frederick Cherrill, *Cherrill of the Yard: The Autobiography of Fred Cherrill* (London: Harrap, 1954). On the contributions of Azizul Haque to the classification scheme associated with Henry's name, see John Berry's essay, 'The History and Development of Fingerprinting', in Henry C. Lea and R. C. Gaensslen (eds), *Advances in Fingerprint Technology* (New York: Elsevier, 1991), pp. 1–38; and S. E. Haylock, 'Khan Bahadur Azizul Haque', *Fingerprint Whorld*, 5, no. 17 (1979): 28–9. Some material of uncertain provenance in the Indian Police Collection at the British Library's Oriental and India Office Collections (Mss Eur F 161/185) supports Haque's claims without any documentary evidence from the period in question. However, three items in this collection are rather more impressive than the rest. The first two are letters to *The Times* from Sir Douglas Gordon and H. C. Mitchell, both of which I have quoted from in this book. The third is an offprint of an article by Shreenivas and Saradindu Narayan Sinha, 'Personal Identification by the Dermatoglyphic and the E-V Methods', *Patna Journal of Medicine*, 31 (1957): 97–108, which claims (on p. 103, without substantiation) that Henry could not initially comprehend Haque's scheme. See also Radhika Singha, 'Settle, Mobilize, Verify: Identification Practices in Colonial India', *Studies in History*, NS 16 (2000): 151–98 (on pp. 181–2), an admirably wide-ranging study of the political significance of identification techniques in colonial India, which discusses Haque's claim in some detail.

On British debates over the identification of habitual offenders, see Leon Radzinowicz and Roger Hood, 'Incapacitating the

Habitual Criminal: The English Experience', *Michigan Law Review*, 78 (1980): 1305–89; and C. E. Troup, A. Griffiths and M. L. Macnaghten, *Report of a Committee appointed by the Secretary of State to Inquire into the Best Means Available for Identifying Habitual Criminals* (Command Paper C-7263), 1894, found most easily in the *House of Commons Parliamentary Papers*, 72 (1893–94): 209–91. The Belper Committee's report (*Report of a Committee appointed by the Secretary of State to Inquire into the Method of Identification of Criminals by Measurements and Finger Prints with Minutes of Evidence and Appendices*, 1901) is available only at the Public Record Office in Kew, London (HO 144/566/A62042/3). The PRO also holds an interesting collection of reports and correspondence on the early use of fingerprinting at Scotland Yard (HO 45/10409/A63109); the confidential report of the War Office Committee on Identification by Finger Prints (WO 33/229); the handwritten evidence and correspondence of that committee (WO 32/8706); correspondence on the fingerprinting of expelled aliens (HO 45/10516/135164) and that on the suggestion to use fingerprints for vetting applicants for naturalization (HO 45/24722). On the British reluctance to introduce national identity cards, see Jon Agar, 'Modern Horrors: British Identity and Identity Cards', in Jane Caplan and John Torpey (eds), *Documenting Individual Identity: The Development of State Practices since the French Revolution* (Princeton, NJ: Princeton University Press, 2001).

On the history of the 1905 Aliens Act and later immigration restrictions, see T. W. E. Roche, *The Key in the Lock: Immigration Control in England from 1066 to the Present Day* (London: John Murray, 1969); Bernard Gainer, *The Alien Invasion: The Origins of the Aliens Act of 1905* (London: Heinemann Educational, 1972); Colin Holmes, *John Bull's Island: Immigration and British Society, 1871–1971* (Basingstoke: Macmillan, 1988); and Ann Dummett and Andrew Nicol, *Subjects, Citizens, Aliens and Others: Nationality and Immigration Law* (London: Weidenfeld and Nicolson, 1990). The *Aliens Order, 1920*, reprinted with subsequent amendments (London: HMSO, 1939, 1948) is well worth examining. The classic account of Victorian openness toward refugees is Bernard Porter, *The Refugee Question in Mid-Victorian Politics* (Cambridge: Cambridge University Press, 1979) On the recent move to fingerprint asylum seekers, see Kamal Ahmed and Jason Burke, 'Asylum Seekers "Must Give Prints"', *Observer*, 9 September 2001, p. 2, col. 8. On the new 'smart cards' for asylum seekers, see http://news.bbc.co.uk/hi/english/uk_politics/newsid_1793000/1793151.stm (accessed on 31 January 2002) and on plans to extend it to all citizens and use them as electronic passports, see http://news.bbc.co.uk/hi/english/uk_politics/newsid_1802000/1802847.stm and http://news.bbc.co.uk/hi/english/uk_politics/newsid_1832000/1832802.stm (both accessed on 21 February 2002). Edward Higgs, 'The Rise of the Information State: The Development of Central State Surveillance of the Citizen in England, 1500–2000', *Journal of Historical Sociology*, 14 (2001): 175–97 is very informative on the rise of a surveillance state in Britain. John Torpey, *The Invention of the Passport: Surveillance, Citizenship and the State* (Cambridge: Cambridge University Press, 2000) shows how the identification of its citizens became a crucial task (and privilege) of the sovereign nation state. Bernard Porter, *The Origins of the Vigilant State* (London: Weidenfeld and Nicolson, 1987) is invaluable on the security question and the Empire's contribution to policing.

The literature on British India is too vast to be even summarized here. There are substantial essays on India with helpful bibliographies in the five volumes of *The Oxford History of the British Empire* (Oxford: Oxford University Press, 1999). Of the countless shorter overviews, Lawrence James, *Raj: The Making and Unmaking of British India* (London: Little, Brown, 1997) is one of the latest. On the cultural aspects of the Indo-British encounter and its broader contexts and outcomes, the chapters on India in V. G. Kiernan, *The Lords of Human Kind: European Attitudes to the Outside World in the Imperial Age* (revised edition; London: Penguin, 1972) have not been superseded. For authentic glimpses into the lives, challenges and opinions of colonial administrators of the nineteenth century, three works are strongly recommended: John Beames, *Memoirs of a Bengal Civilian* (London: Eland, 1984); H. E. A. Cotton, *Indian and Home Memories* (London: Unwin, 1911); and George Otto Trevelyan, *The Competition Wallah*, 2nd edition (London: Macmillan, 1866).

Historians have long appreciated that the illiberal nature of colonial rule permitted the British to introduce innovations in India that would have been impossible or difficult at home, although, oddly, nobody seems to have explored this theme very comprehensively. Eric Stokes, *The English Utilitarians and India* (Oxford: Clarendon Press, 1959) remains a classic analysis but confined to the sphere of law and administration. Although no similarly profound study of scientific work in the Raj is available, there is much illuminating material in Roy M. MacLeod, 'Scientific Advice for British India: Imperial Perceptions and Administrative Goals, 1898–1923', *Modern Asian Studies*, 9 (1975): 343–84; Russell Dionne and Roy MacLeod, 'Science and Policy in British India, 1858–1914: Perspectives on a Persisting Belief', in *Asie du Sud: Traditions et Changements* (*Colloques Internationaux du Centre National de la Recherche Scientifique*, no. 582 [1979]): 55–68; Zaheer Baber, *The Science of Empire: Scientific Knowledge, Civilization, and Colonial Rule in India* (Albany, NY: State University of New York Press, 1996); Deepak Kumar, *Science and the Raj, 1857–1905* (Delhi: Oxford University Press, 1997); and Gyan Prakash, *Another Reason: Science and the Imagination of Modern India* (Princeton, NJ: Princeton University Press, 1999). David Arnold, *Science, Technology and Medicine in Colonial India* (Cambridge:

Cambridge University Press, 2000) is the best single source on the strange but dynamic character of scientific research in British India and Matthew H. Edney, *Mapping an Empire: The Geographical Construction of British India* (Chicago: University of Chicago Press, 1997) is far broader in its conclusions than its title indicates. For more general – but indispensable – analyses of the British Empire's knowledge-gathering projects, see two collections of essays by Bernard Cohn: *An Anthropologist among the Historians and Other Essays* (Delhi: Oxford University Press, 1987) and *Colonialism and its Forms of Knowledge: The British in India* (Princeton, NJ: Princeton University Press, 1996). Nicholas B. Dirks, *Castes of Mind: Colonialism and the Making of Modern India* (Princeton, NJ: Princeton University Press, 2001), although published too late for me to use it extensively, extends Cohn's pathbreaking studies into new areas.

Specifically on colonial anthropology in India, see the succinct account by Christopher Pinney, 'Colonial Anthropology in the "Laboratory of Mankind"', in C. A. Bayly (ed.), *The Raj: India and the British, 1600–1947* (London: Pearson, 1991), pp. 252–63. On the study of race and caste in colonial India, see the essays in Peter Robb (ed.), *The Concept of Race in South Asia* (Delhi: Oxford University Press, 1995) and the essays by Nicholas B. Dirks ('The Crimes of Colonialism: Anthropology and the Textualization of India') and Peter Pels ('The Rise and Fall of the Indian Aborigines: Orientalism, Anglicism, and the Emergence of an Ethnology of India, 1883–1869') in Peter Pels and Oscar Salemink (eds), *Colonial Subjects: Essays on the Practical History of Anthropology* (Ann Arbor, Mich.: University of Michigan Press, 1999), pp. 153–79 and 82–116 respectively. For the undiluted flavour of colonial anthropology and anthropometry, see Sir Herbert Risley's essay on ethnology and caste in *The Imperial Gazetteer of India*, 3rd edition, 26 volumes (Oxford: Clarendon Press, 1907), 1, pp. 283–348, especially pp. 284–91. The whole *Gazetteer* offers an unrivalled panorama of colonial concepts of India and Indians.

For the history of the concept of 'criminal tribe' (and, generally, on policing in colonial India), see David Arnold, *Police Power and Colonial Rule: Madras 1859–1947* (Delhi: Oxford University Press, 1986); Radhika Singha, *A Despotism of Law: Crime and Justice in Early Colonial India* (Delhi: Oxford University Press, 1998); Anand Yang (ed.), *Crime and Criminality in British India* (Tucson, Ariz: University of Arizona Press, 1985); Nicholas B. Dirks, 'The Crimes of Colonialism'; and Sanjay Nigam, 'Disciplining and Policing the "Criminals by Birth", Part 1: The Making of a Colonial Stereotype – The Criminal Tribes and Castes of North India' and '"Disciplining and Policing the "Criminals by Birth", Part 2: The Development of a Disciplinary System', *Indian Economic and Social History Review*, 27 (1990): 131–64; 257–87. On reformatories for criminal tribes, see Rachel J. Tolen, 'Colonizing and Transforming the Criminal Tribesman: The Salvation Army in British India', in Jennifer Terry and Jacqueline Urla (eds), *Deviant Bodies: Critical Perspectives on Difference in Science and Popular Culture* (Bloomington, Ind.: Indiana University Press, 1995), pp. 78–108.

For British concerns with habitual offenders in India, the best source is the 'Papers relating to the Bill for the More Effective Surveillance and Control of Habitual Offenders in India and Certain Connected Purposes', in *Selections from the Records of the Government of India, Home Department*, 300 (Calcutta, 1893; British Library Oriental and India Office Collection MF 1/530–534). On the idea of Indians being naturally dishonest, see Vinay Lal, 'Everyday Crime, Native Mendacity and the Cultural Psychology of Justice in Colonial India', *Studies in History*, NS 15 (1999): 145–66. For trenchant samples of authoritative British views on native mendacity, see Norman Chevers, *A Manual of Medical Jurisprudence for India, includ-*

ing the Outline of a History of Crime against the Person in India (Calcutta: Thacker, Spink, 1870), pp. 75–6, 85–6, 100; P. Heher and J. D. B. Gribble, *Outlines of Medical Jurisprudence for India*, 5th edition (Madras: Higginbotham, 1908), pp. 28–9, 33; and L. A. Waddell, *Lyon's Medical Jurisprudence for India with Illustrative Cases*, 5th edition (Calcutta: Thacker, Spink, 1914), p. 19.

Of the early cases involving fingerprint evidence in India, see *'Queen Empress v.: 1. Fakir Mahomed Sheikh, 2. Arshad Ali Shaha, 3. Sitanath'*, *Calcutta Weekly Notes: Law Notes and Notes of Important Decisions of the Calcutta High Court and of Appeals to the Judicial Committee of the Privy Council*, 1 (1896–97): 33–5 and on the subsequent debates on the change of the Indian law on admissibility of expert evidence: 'Expert Evidence on Finger-Impressions', *Calcutta Weekly Notes*, 3 (1898–99): iv, xxiv, lxxxii–lxxxiii. See also *'Emperor v. Abdul Hamid'*, *Indian Law Reports, Calcutta Series*, 32 (1905): 759–70; *'Emperor v. Sahdeo'*, *Nagpur Law Reports*, 3 (1907): 1–19; and the account of the Man Singh murder case in I. B. Lyon, *Medical Jurisprudence for India with Illustrative Cases*, 3rd edition revised and updated by L. A. Waddell (Calcutta: Thacker, Spink, 1904), pp. 49–51 (the previously cited 5th edition omits crucial passages). For the Indian Evidence Act and a commentary on the admissibility of expert evidence on fingerprint identification, see John George Woodroffe and Frank James Mathew, *Woodroffe and Ameer Ali's Law of Evidence Applicable to British India*, 3rd edition (Calcutta: Thacker, Spink, 1911), pp. 401, 408–9.

On forgery of fingerprints in India, see Henry Smith, 'The Forging of Finger-Prints and Seals and the Remedy', *Transactions of the Medico-Legal Society (London)*, 24 (1931): 87–93, followed by discussion, pp. 93–101 and F. Brewester, *Fingerprints: The Numerical Index or, Fingerprints Revolutionised* (Calcutta: Eastern Law House, 1936), pp. 163–82. On the issue of fingerprint forgery in general, see the classic detective novel by R. Austin Freeman, *The Red Thumb Mark* (New York: Dover, 1986; originally published in 1907) in which the legendary medical jurist and detective Dr John Evelyn Thorndyke made his debut. For a detailed, unequivocal dismissal of the possibility of forging fingerprints that would deceive an expert, see B. C. Bridges, *Practical Fingerprinting* (New York: Funk and Wagnalls, 1942), pp. 293–8. A recent (and somewhat less dismissive) review of the topic is available in Boris Geller, Joseph Almog, Pierre Margot and Eliot Springer, 'A Chronological Review of Fingerprint Forgery', *Journal of Forensic Sciences*, 44 (1999): 963–8.

Harry Jackson's trial is mentioned in most histories of fingerprinting, but the most detailed report was in *Daily Telegraph*, 15 September 1902 (clipping in PRO HO 45/10409/A63109/10). On the Deptford murders, see the reports in *The Times*, 6 May 1905, p. 19, cols 1–2 and 8 May 1905, p. 4, cols 4–6. On the life and career of counsel Richard Muir, who played such an important role in both trials, see Sidney Theodore Felstead, *Sir Richard Muir: A Memoir of a Public Prosecutor. Intimate Revelations compiled from the Papers of Sir Richard Muir, Late Senior Counsel to the British Treasury, edited by Lady Muir* (London: John Lane, 1927).

Index

The index covers the Introduction, Chapters 1–6, the Conclusion and the Appendix. Illustrations are indicated by page numbers in *italic*, e.g. Henry, Edward Richard 2, 86, *115*, *123*. Titles of books and journals are in *italic*, e.g. *The Adventure of the Norwood Builder* (Doyle) 167. Definitions and explanations are given in **bold**, e.g. Belper Committee **172**.

INDEX

UNIVERSITY OF WINCHESTER
LIBRARY

MIRANDA CARTER

Anthony Blunt

His Lives

PAN BOOKS

Winner of the Orwell Prize 2001 and
The Royal Society of Literature Award 2001

When Anthony Blunt died in 1983, he was a man about whom almost anything could be – and was – said. As Surveyor of the Queen's Pictures and Director of the Courtauld Institute, Blunt's position was assured until his exposure in 1979 left his reputation in tatters. Miranda Carter's brilliantly insightful biography gives us a vivid portrait of a human paradox. Blunt's totally discrete lives, with their permanent contradictions, serve to remind us that there is no one key to any human being's identity: we are all a series of conflicting selves.

'Highly impressive . . . sensitive and compelling'
Noel Malcolm, *Sunday Telegraph*

'Immediately establishes her as one of Britain's most promising young biographers . . . Admirable'
The Times

'A minatory masterpiece'
Guardian

ALEX KERSHAW

Blood and Champagne

The Life and Times of Robert Capa

PAN BOOKS

*'A fine read, full of high emotion, like watching
Casablanca for the first time. A tale rich with intrigue,
love, lust, lies and betrayal . . . I loved this book'*
Janine di Giovanni, Literary Review

Photographer Robert Capa's work during the Spanish Civil War and
the Second World War made him a legend. He was killed in Indo-
China in 1954, among the earliest casualties of what would become
the Vietnam War. Friend of Hemingway, Gary Cooper, Gene Kelly,
John Huston, and lover of Ingrid Bergman, Capa is one of the great
figures of the twentieth century, and Alex Kershaw's story of his life
is every bit as dramatic as the pictures he took.

'Ambition, integrity and courage were intertwined in Capa,
as Alex Kershaw persuades in this elegant biography . . .
a spellbinding portrait of his gypsy life'
Sunday Times

'Packed with good stories, and snappily written,
Blood and Champagne is as full of life as the man it celebrates'
Observer

'Remarkably fine'
Daily Telegraph

DIANE ATKINSON

Love & Dirt

The Marriage of Arthur Munby & Hannah Cullwick

PAN BOOKS

'A fascinating love affair'
Sunday Times

Arthur Munby, barrister and published poet, met Hannah Cullwick, Shropshire scullery maid, on London's Oxford Street in 1854. Their encounter was the beginning of a clandestine love affair that was to last, in fierce defiance of Victorian barriers of class, for over fifty years. Fuelling the couple's attraction was a bizarre mutual obsession. Munby, long fascinated by working women, adored watching Hannah 'in her dirt' going about her work, and Hannah responded to him with a literally slavish devotion. Both were avid writers of letters and diaries, and Diane Atkinson has drawn on their legacy to tell the captivating story of a forbidden love, and a relationship as enduring as it was extraordinary.

'Shadowy figures at the edge of Victorian life,
they might almost have stepped out of a Dickens plot'
Claire Tomalin, *Evening Standard*

'Arthur and Hannah have been lucky with their biographer . . .
Diane Atkinson has a generous appreciation of all the nuances and
paradoxes of their bizarre relationship'
Craig Brown, *Mail on Sunday*

OTHER BOOKS

AVAILABLE FROM PAN MACMILLAN

MIRANDA CARTER
ANTHONY BLUNT   0 330 36766 8   £8.99

ALEX KERSHAW
BLOOD AND CHAMPAGNE   0 330 49250 0   £8.99

DIANE ATKINSON
LOVE AND DIRT   0 330 39228 X   £8.99

SUSAN GRIFFIN
THE BOOK OF THE COURTESANS   0 330 48807 4   £7.99

All Pan Macmillan titles can be ordered from our website,
www.panmacmillan.com, or from your local bookshop
and are also available by post from:

Bookpost, PO Box 29, Douglas, Isle of Man IM99 1BQ
Credit cards accepted. For details:
Telephone: 01624 677237
Fax: 01624 670923
E-mail: bookshop@enterprise.net
www.bookpost.co.uk

Free postage and packing in the United Kingdom

Prices shown above were correct at the time of going to press.
Pan Macmillan reserve the right to show new retail prices on covers
which may differ from those previously advertised in the text
or elsewhere.